STRAIGHT TALK

STRAIGHTALK

LISA STADLER

**YOUR ISSUES
YOUR PROBLEMS
YOUR SOLUTIONS**

CF4·K

© Copyright 2007 Lisa Stadler

ISBN 978-1-84550-260-7

Published in 2007 by

Christian Focus Publications,

Geanies House, Fearn, Tain

Ross-shire, IV20 1TW, Great Britain

Cover design by Danie van Straaten

Cover illustrations by Jeff Anderson

Printed and Bound by CPD, Wales

American spelling is used throughout the book.

Scripture taken from the New King James Version.

Copyright © 1982 by Thomas Nelson, Inc.

Used by permission.

All rights reserved. No part of this publication may be reproduced, stored in a retrieval system, or transmitted, in any form, by any means, electronic, mechanical, photocopying, recording or otherwise without the prior permission of the publisher or a license permitting restricted copying. In the U.K. such licenses are issued by the Copyright Licensing Agency, 90 Tottenham Court Road, London W1P 9HE.

Dedicated to Gabriella Renee
– my greatest gift in this world.
"Let no one despise your youth, but be an example to the believers in word, in conduct, in love, in spirit, in faith, in purity" 1 Timothy 4:12.

CONTENTS

Point me to the exit sign! 9

Is it OK with God? 13

Holiday heartache 25

I'll never be a twig 35

I didn't want to move 45

Personal space? What's that?! 55

No time for God 63

That used to be my job! 71

But he's not my real father 83

Why wait? 93

Sometimes I try to split them up 101

Burger or bubble? 113

Mom lets me do it 121

Cut and run 133

Stuck in the middle 145

Make way for baby 155

Wearing dirty laundry 165

The party's over 177

POINT ME TO THE EXIT SIGN!

Life is crazy. Just when you think that you have something figured out — or at least that everything is going OK for the moment — that's when things get messed up again.

With a lot of effort, you may be able to control your own emotions and actions. Unfortunately, you can't force other people to respond the way that you want. Human emotions can be so unpredictable, and that is what makes relationships so tough.

But emotions are not the only problem. Today, being a teen is a lot like walking through a funhouse. At the entrance to the funhouse you see crazy, distorted mirrors. Just as these mirrors are distorted, the world does a great job of distorting truth. Movies, music and video games make crime and promiscuity seem really cool. The Internet is full of predators who pretend to be teens. Schools teach that 'tolerance' means 'no definite wrong and right for all people.'

Next in the funhouse, you come to the spinning barrel. You know the path that God wants you to take; if you just look straight ahead, you won't fall. But instead of walking straight ahead, you begin to wonder: Just how far to the right or the left can I walk without falling down?

Now you've come to the next room in the funhouse — the giant mirror maze. The room is filled with images that look like you — but which one is really you? It should be easy to figure out – but somehow, it's not. When you were younger you felt more certain about what you believed in ... at least, you were sure of what your parents taught you to believe. But lately you've been questioning those beliefs. Shouldn't 'right and wrong' depend on the person, or the situation? Is the answer to everything really in the Bible?

Being a Christian teen does not automatically shield you from mirrors and mazes. It is completely OK for you to have questions and concerns about life, just like your non-Christian friends do. You may feel disappointed, sad or angry at times. And on some days, you will mess up. After all, being a Christian is still being a human.

POINT ME TO THE EXIT SIGN!

Even if you're not a Christian, you can still read this book. You need God's advice and his Word whether you believe in him or not. Perhaps you'll find yourself wanting to find out more about God – that's good. He wants to talk to you and reason things out with you. Throughout this book you are encouraged to get into God's word – and that's exactly the place for you to go to find out about God and Jesus Christ.

Just like anybody else, Christians make mistakes. But we have guidelines for figuring out the answers. Did you realize that everything you need to know about life and relationships is in the Bible? Even the answers to your toughest problems can be found there. They may not always be easy to follow – still, the answers are there if you are willing to find them.

This devotional will show you how to find those answers. Each chapter deals with a specific issue that teens face. The first section in each chapter tells a story of a teen who has run into that problem. Next there is a section called Thinking it Through. This section will help you tackle that issue in your own life. The section called Talking With God is a prayer that you may want to use in that type of situation.

Even if you are not going through a particular issue at the moment, chances are that you have a friend who is. Or you may need some advice on this issue later on. Either way, the Making Connections section will give you some solid advice.

At the end of each chapter, you will find some Scripture verses related to that issue. God doesn't want you to be like a robot, just believing certain things because somebody told you it was true. He really likes it when you use your brain to search for the answers yourself – by reading the Bible. The verses in each chapter will get you started on that search for truth.

Even when you know God's answers to your problems, life can be tricky. Many times, relationships still hurt. But isn't it great to know that the Lord is on your side, giving you the strength to work through things?

As you read this book, you will feel more peace, trust and strength each day. When you have a rough day, remember to lean on God. As you begin to strengthen your relationship with Him, you will begin to grow more strength to deal with life – no matter what may be around the next corner of that funhouse!

"Let my cry come before You, O LORD; Give me understanding according to Your Word," Psalm 119:169.

IS IT OK WITH GOD?

Ryan dreaded walking into youth group. Normally he liked being around his friends. And Pastor Steve was always cool. His talks were a total reality check; but he also knew how to have fun. Up until now, church was a good place to be. Up until now, he hadn't known that Dad was cheating on Mom.

Two months ago, Dad told Ryan that he would be moving out soon. This was really no big surprise. His parents had been fighting non-stop for the past year, so Ryan figured there was a chance they'd split up. Dad said that he loved Mom, but they just didn't see things the same way.

Mom had a different take on the whole thing. "Don't

worry, Ryan. Things aren't over yet. God can fix the marriage if we both try really hard."

Dad left a few days later, saying that he would be staying with a friend from college. He said that Mom and Ryan could reach him on his cell phone if they needed anything.

Ryan noticed that Dad didn't take any big stuff with him — just a suitcase. *Maybe he's not planning on being gone long*, Ryan thought hopefully.

It helped to talk about things with his friends at church. Ryan's friends really liked Dad, and so did Pastor Steve. Dad was always there if a snowboarding or river-rafting trip was happening. When it came to outdoor fun, he was hard-core. Dad also spent a lot of time talking to the kids.

The youth group prayed every week for Ryan's parents to work things out. Pastor Steve told Ryan that he thought things would be OK. "I know your dad loves the Lord. He'll figure things out with your mom."

Then Dad stopped coming to church. Ryan knew that wasn't a good sign. Mom seemed to feel it too. She told Ryan that Dad did not want to go to counseling. Still, she reassured her son that God could make things OK. "God created marriage, and He hates divorce. I'll just keep trying to show Dad how much I love him."

IS IT OK WITH GOD?

One Sunday, Pastor Steve had an idea. "Hey, Ry — how about if I spend some time with your dad? We get along well. Maybe he would trust me enough to talk about things."

Ryan wasn't so sure. If Dad wasn't coming to church, then would he really want to talk to a pastor? He thought maybe he should run it by his father first.

"I'll talk to him, and then I'll let you know what he said," Ryan replied.

"Sounds like a plan," agreed Pastor Steve. "See you on Tuesday night."

When Ryan got home, he dialed Dad's cell number. A woman answered. *Must've dialed wrong*, Ryan thought. He hung up and redialed slowly.

Again the same woman answered, this time with an annoyed tone in her voice: *"Yes?"*

What should I do now? Ryan wondered. "Uh, yeah, I was looking for my dad, Greg. Do I have the wrong number?"

The woman sounded embarrassed. "Oh. Yes ... this is his number."

"Then why are you answering his phone?" asked Ryan.

"Because he's in the shower," answered Mystery Woman.

15

"Well, who *are* you anyway?" demanded Ryan, as a huge knot formed in his stomach.

"I ... we're ... well, your dad can explain it to you better," she stammered.

Ryan was not going to let her off that easy. "Wait a minute ... so Dad is staying with *you*?! He told Mom that he was staying with his friend from college!"

Mystery Woman was really nervous now. "Look, I don't know what he's told you. I don't want to get in the middle of anything here, so ..."

Ryan interrupted, "You don't want to get in the *middle*?! Wrecking someone's marriage kinda falls in the category of 'getting in the middle', don't you think?!"

"Look, I don't want to get into this with you. Talk to Greg about it, alright?" she said anxiously.

Ryan hung up on her. *Oh, I'll talk to Greg about it – don't you worry*, thought Ryan furiously.

Dad called back ten minutes later. "Son, I am so sorry you found out about Donna this way."

"*Donna?*" Ryan shouted. "Dad, let's not even give her a name in this conversation, because I have a few stronger names in mind for her."

"Ryan! You should not speak about her that way. She's done nothing to you," Dad answered firmly.

"What cloud did you fall off of? Wake up and listen

to yourself! You have a wife. Maybe you and Mom have some major problems, but she is a great woman and she loves you. You don't even deserve her!"

"Watch your mouth, Son!"

Ryan knew he was over the top now; but he couldn't seem to stop. "I guess that wasn't good enough for you. No wonder you haven't shown your face at church. It's because you know that God hates what you're doing. And so do I."

Silence from Dad. Then finally he answered in a defeated voice, "Hey, Ry, I'm sorry. Truly sorry. But sometimes things just don't work out. Your mother and I tried ..."

Ryan interrupted him. "No, Dad. *Mom* tried. She even wanted to go to counseling with you, but you wouldn't do it. You just took the easy way out. Or should I say, the sleazy way?"

"*Ryan!* That is enough!"

"Dad, haven't you always taught me that Christians can't just pick and choose which of God's laws they want to obey, and which ones they don't? That should include marriage, shouldn't it? *Your* marriage, Dad."

Dad did not appreciate the lecture. "Ryan, you may not agree with what I'm doing, but that does not give you the right to talk to me disrespectfully!"

Ryan couldn't believe what he was hearing. "Dad, you expect me to treat you with respect – yet at the same time, you are disrespecting my mother. Interesting."

"Ryan, you're totally out of line right now. I'll talk to you when you've had time to calm down," Dad said angrily as he hung up.

Now it was Tuesday night. Youth group would be starting in a few minutes. Everyone would be asking Ryan how things were going with his parents. Even worse, Pastor Steve would want to know how the phone conversation went.

How was Ryan supposed to tell them that his father was not the great guy they thought he was? Greg the role model was nothing but a fake. Ryan had never been so ashamed in his life.

THINKING IT THROUGH

Teens today face more temptation than ever. It helps to have a good adult role model to count on; someone who will listen when you are down, or influence you to make wise choices when you are confused. In Ryan's case that person was his father, Greg.

Ryan's friends saw his dad as a role model too. Greg showed a real interest in their lives. He was there to listen when they wanted to talk, and he liked being a part of their fun.

It must have been hard on Ryan to hear his parents fighting all the time. It could not have been easy to hear that they would separate. But Ryan's faith in his dad's character helped him deal with the situation. Greg had always seemed to be a godly man. Ryan was sure his dad would eventually work things out with his mom.

It hurts when a parent does not live up to your expectations. After all, they are the adults — aren't they the ones who are supposed to be setting the example?

Separation and divorce are hard enough to handle; but how do you deal with it when you find out that your parent has committed adultery?

You are sure that breaking a commandment is *not* going to go over big with God. It makes no sense. Your whole life, your parents have taught you to obey God's laws. But now one of your parents is breaking God's law, big-time.

How can you trust this parent? How can you just watch them do what they are doing, when you know it is wrong?

Will you have to accept another person as your stepparent some day? What will your friends think? Most of all, what does God think?

Tough questions. Let's start with God, since He is the

one who made the rule book. There's no way around it. God is never OK with adultery, period. God created marriage to be a relationship with only one person, permanently. One of the Ten Commandments specifically says: "*You shall not commit adultery.*" Adultery not only dishonors the marriage partner; it dishonors God. Does God forgive your parent for committing adultery? God can forgive His children for anything. He truly *wants* to forgive. The Scriptures tell us that He is our *Abba* – our loving Dad. But He does require one thing to happen first – repentance.

Repentance is more than just saying 'I'm sorry'. It means that a person truly *feels* sorry, and believes that they have done wrong. It also means that they intend to change the way they live, to *show* that they are sorry.

The hard part is, you can't *make* your parent repent. You can hope for it, pray for it, and even try to convince them to do it. But in the end it is a choice that can only be made by your parent.

Keep in mind that as much as you may disagree with a parent's behavior, this does not give you the right to tell them off. True, your parent has broken a commandment. But if you respond disrespectfully, you will be no better off than they are, because then you too will be breaking a commandment: "*Honor Your Father and Your Mother*".

If you do decide to have a heart-to-heart with your parent, pray about it first. Ask God to help you present your point in a calm, respectful way. Show loving concern for your parent, but do not scold them. And afterwards, keep praying that they will consider your words carefully.

Your friends will know that your parent has done something wrong – just as you already do. They may feel shock and disappointment, even sadness that this has happened to someone they care about. But if they are truly your friends, they will not treat you any differently; it is certainly not your fault that this has happened.

Still, prepare yourself. There will always be people who turn out to be shallow. When times are happy, they are your best friends. But when you need them in a crisis, they run away or gossip about your problems.

Unfortunately, there are people like this everywhere – even in church. So do not let these people get the best of you. God sees what they are really like, and He will correct them in His own way.

Beyond that, you've got to let go. Keep praying for everyone involved. But the answer is in God's hands. He will give you the strength and the wisdom you need to deal with the outcome, no matter what it is.

STRAIGHTTALK

TALKING WITH GOD

Dear Father, I am tempted to show disrespect to my parent for what they have done; but I know that is not what You want. Help me to find a way to love and respect my parent in spite of the choices they are making right now. I pray that my true friends will help me through this. Amen.

MAKING CONNECTIONS

Think about how many pop stars are considered role models, simply because they are attractive and they can sing. Consider how many male athletes are called role models. True, they may have trained hard to reach the top, but once they are there, some athletes seem more concerned with money and women than with the game itself. You may not know for sure whether a celebrity is a Christian or not, but you can definitely tell a lot about them by their words and actions. What is the message they are sending out? Do they show respect for others – or is it all about them? If their lifestyle is a spiritual train wreck, then they are not role models at all. Do a web search to find out which athletes are Christians, and research their stories. Have any magazines interviewed your favorite Christian singers? What hard times have these people been through, and how has God helped

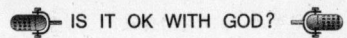

them? If they have gotten through life with God's strength – then so can you.

DIGGING DEEPER

"Honor your father and your mother, that your days may be long upon the land which the LORD your God is giving you," *Exodus 20:12*.

"You shall not commit adultery," *Exodus 20:14*.

"He who covers his sins will not prosper, but whoever confesses and forsakes them will have mercy," *Proverbs 28:13*.

HOLIDAY HEARTACHE

Ever since her mother died two years ago, Rachel dreaded Christmas. Rachel and Dad had learned to deal with it, and they had bonded closer together as a result. But on the inside, Rachel's heart felt like a tornado.

She felt really angry at her friends. It seemed as if they expected Rachel to just get over her mother's death. They never really understood what she was going through. How could they? Their mothers were still around.

In a strange way, Rachel's frustration was also directed at Mom. *Why did she have to leave us like that?! Everything was fine when we were all together.* Rachel knew that it didn't make any sense to be mad at Mom, because Mom didn't *choose* to die. But then again, nothing in her life made sense these days.

More than anyone else, Rachel was mad at God for letting Mom die in the first place. She had prayed so hard that Mom would get better. But God took her away instead. The one person she was not angry at was Dad. It wasn't his fault that Mom died. Dad didn't want Mom gone any more than Rachel did.

Now that Dad had gotten remarried, there was someone new for Rachel to be angry at: her stepmother, Lori. *That woman will never understand what Dad and I have been through*, Rachel thought bitterly. *She wasn't even around.*

Rachel heard holiday music coming from the kitchen. Lori was rattling bowls and dishes. She was also singing in a cheerful voice, " ... *so have a Merry Christmas!*"

Rachel cringed. *Merry? As if.*

"Rachel? Is that you, Hun?"

Hun?! I am not your Hun, Rachel thought irritably. *It was OK for Mom to call me that, but not you.*

"Yeah, it's me," said Rachel.

"I'm so glad you're home!" gushed Lori. "I have a surprise for you."

Rachel immediately felt a wall go up in her heart. She silently answered her stepmother in her mind: *OK, Lori – let's get something straight:*

A. This is MY home, not yours. You just happened to

move in when you married Dad; and

B. Whatever surprise you have for me, I'm sure I'm not interested.

Rachel said nothing out loud. Her stepmother anxiously waited for Rachel to ask about the surprise. Instead, Rachel just rolled her eyes and waited for Lori to tell her.

"Rach, I found these cookie kits today; we can make our own gingerbread houses! I even bought different kinds of candy to decorate them. What do you think?" asked Lori hopefully.

Actually, Rachel thought it sounded like fun – and she knew it would make Dad happy to see her working on something with Lori. But for some reason, she didn't want her stepmom to know that she liked her idea.

"Cool," she said, with a bored expression on her face. Then she walked away.

She sat down on the sofa and checked out the scenery. There were Christmas decorations everywhere. Rachel scowled. *These obnoxious things must be Lori's.* She especially hated the ugly wreath that Lori had hung on the front door. It was a big fat reminder that Christmas was never going to be the same.

Thankfully, one or two of the older decorations were still around that had belonged to Rachel and Dad. But even these things weren't in the places where she and Dad usually put them. Lori hadn't even bothered to ask for Rachel's input — she had decorated the whole house while Rachel was at school.

"Where are all the other decorations?" she called out to her stepmom.

"Oh, they were really worn out. I tossed them," Lori answered. "We'll buy a few new ones to replace them."

Sure. Just replace them. Kind of like you're trying to replace Mom, Rachel thought bitterly.

She wondered if Dad had told Lori about their traditions for Christmas dinner. *Probably not,* Rachel decided. *He seems to be OK with letting her do whatever she wants this Christmas. Well, I'm not OK with it.*

Rachel walked back into the kitchen, determined to be heard. "Hey, Lori," she began in a challenging voice.

"What, Hun?"

Ouch. There was that '*Hun*' again.

"Dad and I have some traditions for Christmas dinner," she announced. "We always cook a ham, and we make mashed potatoes the way my grandma used to do it. Those are the only kind Dad eats, so it has to be done the right way. We have peas and corn too. We also buy an apple pie — and it has to be a certain brand — and two kinds of ice cream for dessert."

Lori was blown away. After the shock wore off, she finally said, "That sounds like a really nice Christmas dinner, Rach. But I've already planned something else for dinner. I really think you're going to like it."

This was definitely *not* the response Rachel was looking for.

How could Lori think it was perfectly fine to dump all the traditions?! Who elected her Christmas Queen?

Rachel let her stepmom know exactly how she felt. "Look, Lori – Dad's not gonna be happy that you've trashed our plans. He likes things a certain way. Maybe you just don't get that yet, because you haven't been around as long as I have. But here's a little F.Y.I. – he won't like it that you're changing the dinner – and neither do I."

Lori's face was as red as a chili pepper. Rachel was glad that her stepmom was losing it. *Good! Welcome to my world!* she thought. *How does it feel?* But she was not expecting Lori's reply. It hit her like a brick.

"Rachel," she began in a serious tone – all the 'Hun' now gone from her voice – "thanks for the F.Y.I.; now here's one for you. Your dad knows about the dinner I've planned. In fact, he *helped me* plan it. We were trying to start a fun tradition, since we are a new family now. But it's kind of obvious that you don't see it that way.

So if you're through condemning me for today, I've got some things to do."

The angry ache in Rachel's heart grew more painful at that moment than it had ever felt before. Her father had betrayed her! She added him to the list of people who had let her down.

She had no one left to talk to. Nobody could understand things the way she needed them to. Rachel had been angry for so long – and at so many people – that now she was beginning to feel numb.

THINKING IT THROUGH

It's a scary feeling to be walking around with a heart full of rage. You become a time bomb, ready to blow up at any given moment. Anyone in your path becomes a casualty, including friends and family.

Instead of dealing with her feelings about her mom's death, Rachel chose to bury them. Unfortunately that never works; the feelings have to come out somehow. So eventually, Rachel's emotions turned into a dangerous anger that poisoned her heart.

Anger itself is not necessarily harmful. It is a human emotion, just like happiness or sadness. God understands this — He gave you emotions when He created you. It is what you do about your anger that makes it either helpful

HOLIDAY HEARTACHE

or harmful.

To change your heart from poisonous to positive, you will need to do some anger management. Anger management is like a puzzle. You will need to make sure that you have certain pieces to this puzzle in place.

The first piece is *communication*. Have you made your feelings clear to the person who has upset you? If they are clueless about their role in the problem, then it's not fair to expect them to help you solve it. You've got to give that person a chance; talk to them about it.

The next piece is *presentation*. What words or actions have you used to protest? Do your actions help solve the problem, or add to it? Name-calling and accusations cause trouble, but peaceful words can bring positive results.

The last piece is *motive*. Why are you angry or frustrated? Is your anger for righteous reasons? For example, has someone disrespected God, or wronged you, or hurt someone important to you? Or is your anger for selfish reasons? Sometimes people use anger as a way to 'punish' someone for hurting them. Others are angry because they have chosen not to forgive, or they refuse to admit their own faults in a situation.

Once you have carefully considered the pieces that make up your puzzle, think about which pieces are missing. This is the way you will begin putting your heart back together.

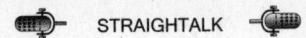 STRAIGHTTALK

Of course, once your heart is reassembled you will need to use some glue to stop things falling apart.

What is this glue? It is a mixture of talking and listening to God. You must talk to Him each day, and pray for the strength to conquer your anger. Listen to His directions each day by reading the Bible.

After awhile, you will begin to see that it is definitely possible to let go of the poison in your heart. Once you've released the heavy anger and bitterness there will be lots more room for joy. Joy feels so much lighter. What a relief!

TALKING WITH GOD

Dear God, I am exhausted from feeling so angry all the time. I have been feeling this way for so long that I don't know how to let it go. Will you please teach me how to feel joy again? I can't do it without You. Help me learn to listen and talk to You every day. Amen.

MAKING CONNECTIONS

Maybe you see yourself as the peaceful one in your family. It seems as if someone else has the anger management problem and for some reason, it is often directed at you. It hurts when someone is always yelling at you. God does not want any of us to be treated that way. If your brother or sister treats you this way, talk about the anger issue before it happens again. Choose a peaceful time to tell this person what is on your mind. Keep your voice calm and your words polite. Explain how you feel, using "I" statements. For example, "I feel hurt when you yell at me" will help the other person to know what your world feels like. But throwing out an accusation like "You are always such a hothead" may ignite more trouble. Anger will not solve anger. If you really want to make progress, leave your spears behind.

DIGGING DEEPER

"Then Jesus went into the temple of God and drove out all those who bought and sold in the temple, and overturned the tables of the money changers and the seats of those who sold doves. And He said to them, "It is written, 'My house shall be called a house of prayer,' but you have made it a 'den of thieves.'" *Matthew 21:12-13*.

"Direct my steps by Your word, and let no iniquity have dominion over me," *Psalm 119:133*.

"To everything there is a season, a time for every purpose under heaven ... a time to weep and a time to laugh; a time to mourn, and a time to dance," *Ecclesiastes 3:1,4*.

I'LL NEVER BE A TWIG

I wonder what to wear tomorrow night, Nicole thought as she doodled in her science notebook. She needed something that would really turn people's heads at the school dance. Nicole always felt so plain next to the cheerleaders and the girls whose daddies bought them whatever they wanted.

She knew that she would never look like those girls anyway. Her mother always said that Nicole was not fat, just 'full-figured' – whatever that meant. She would never fit into their clothes, even if she was on a diet for a million years. They all looked like skinny little twigs, ready to break when the next strong gust of wind hit.

They all had perfect hair too. The rich girls got their

long hair highlighted, straightened or permed to perfection. But Nicole's hair was thick and ridiculously curly. Even if she got it highlighted — which of course her parents couldn't afford — the highlights would be hidden in her big nest of hair.

She could ask her friend Dana if she could borrow something. Dana was a crack-up, which made her popular with everyone — guys and girls. Although Dana's body was definitely not in the twig category, she had a serious wardrobe. Her clothes were trendy, and often left nothing to the imagination.

Unfortunately, those clothes would never pass inspection at Nicole's house.

As she pushed a strand of her wild hair behind her ear, Nicole began to come up with a plan. She would leave her house wearing something her father would OK. Then she'd walk over to Dana's house and change clothes.

"Nicole, perhaps you could join us for science class today," her teacher accused. He had suddenly appeared next to her desk, peering down at the doodling which sprawled across the page where her notes should be.

The whole class turned toward Nicole, laughing and whispering to each other. Some of the whispers were meant to be heard. Jessica Barnes, a cheerleader, made a particularly rude comment: "Maybe she's thinking about all the guys who won't ask to dance with her fat little body."

Yeah, or maybe I'm thinking about how ugly you are as soon as you open your mouth, Miss Twig, Nicole answered her silently.

The next day, Nicole left her house wearing a bulky sweater and an embarrassingly long skirt. Her father told her she looked beautiful, which was really pushing it on the exaggeration scale. She walked quickly to Dana's. Dana rushed her into the house. "Hurry up, Nic! We don't have all night," she complained.

First Dana brought out some huge hot rollers, to tame the wild beast that was Nicole's hair. Next Dana painted Nicole's nails bright blue, with glitter. She wasn't thrilled about that, but Dana made her laugh until she got her way – as usual.

Finally Nicole searched Dana's closet, which actually looked more like a landfill. Every shirt Dana owned was low-cut, and every pair of pants or skirt was designed to fit like an ultra-tight glove. Dana handed Nicole a skimpy purple shirt and a pair of jeans that looked like they would fit a six-year-old. Then she shoved a pair of lethal heels at her.

"Come on, Dana ... my feet will be screaming by the end of the night!" Nicole complained.

But Dana insisted. "We are in competition with the Skinny Patrol. We need ammunition."

Dana took out the curlers and worked an entire handful of gel through Nicole's hair, pulling it hard to keep the frizz from surfacing. Then she ruthlessly plucked Nicole's thick eyebrows.

"Are you trying to kill me?" Nicole whined.

"No pain, no gain. This is how hotties are made," Dana explained.

Nicole looked in the mirror. Between the hair gel and the ton of make-up that Dana had applied, Nicole felt ten pounds heavier. Her nails were blinding her, and her feet were already swelling up. Was it really worth it?

But that wasn't what bothered Nicole most. It was the clothing. Or lack of it, actually. Her pants sat ultra-low on her hips; in fact, her hips actually showed, along with her stomach. Her shirt revealed an embarrassing amount of cleavage.

"Now the boys will finally notice you — in a good way!" Dana said suggestively.

Maybe she's right — that's the only way they'll ever pay attention to me, thought Nicole gloomily. But would it really be 'in a good way'?

THINKING IT THROUGH

What a strange world. The prettiest, thinnest or richest people are not always the nicest. Yet they are often treated much better than the average person. Why? And what is it that draws us to be more like these people?

Flip through any magazine and you will see gorgeous people with perfect teeth, smiling as if they are the happiest humans on the planet. Notice how you don't find any ordinary-looking people in the ads. Turn on the TV, and the same is true. There are beautiful people in the programs, as well as the commercials.

Now look out your window. Hmmm. Interesting how most of the people walking by on the street do not look like the people in the media!

Outward qualities are not important to God. Of course, back in the days of the Bible people did not have TV and magazines. So they didn't have to deal with beauty, popularity and power ... right?

Actually, they did. Although their standards were a bit different, people were still divided into groups like 'popular' and 'outcast.' Take Hannah, for instance. Hannah was married to a guy named Elkanah. They were in love, so life was good. Except ... Hannah couldn't have a baby. No big deal, you may be thinking. But it was huge in Hannah's day. At that time in Israel, a woman who could not have a baby was a total outcast. People probably talked about her all the time — maybe even right in front of her – just like Jessica, the cheerleader who insulted Nicole.

What was worse for Hannah was that her husband had a second wife, Peninnah. That had to be a major blow to her ego. On top of that, Peninnah was able to have babies — lots of them. She constantly teased Hannah for not being able to have a child. Hannah was definitely a girl with a self-image problem.

Another example of the ancient 'in crowd' is the Pharisees, a group of Jews who thought they were above everyone else. The Pharisees were experts at tearing people down. They wore special clothing and accessories as if they were billboards, announcing that they were better Jews than everyone else. The Pharisees talked down to 'regular' people. They also liked to point out how well they kept God's laws.

There was just one problem — the Pharisees really weren't living the way God wanted them to. They had God's laws memorized, but they weren't showing God's love to anyone. In fact, the Pharisees often insulted Jesus and tried to turn people against Him. Sound like anyone you know?

Like the Pharisees, Peninnah, or even Jessica, people

who rely on looks, money or power to get through life do not truly know God. They become so focused on their outer appearance that they are blind to the ugliness inside of them. They begin to care more about popularity or power than relationships.

But the truth is, people like that are insecure on the inside. They know that they can't be number one forever. Without their power or looks they have nothing to offer. Tearing others down helps them avoid dealing with their own issues.

Hannah must have struggled with envy and anger that she couldn't have her own child. She was sick and tired of Peninnah's rude comments. Her own husband did not understand her problems.

That's enough to cause anyone to have a meltdown.

Hannah had a good, long cry and prayed to God with all of her heart. Afterwards, Hannah felt much better. She had asked God to help her, and she believed that He would. As it turned out, God answered her prayers beyond what she asked for. Hannah did have a son – then she had five more children!

At times it is hard not to envy someone else. But envy will never change what you look like on the outside. Instead it will destroy you on the inside. Envy can turn into anger, bitterness and resentment. When you constantly wish that you were someone else, it's as if you are saying that you know better than God what your life should be like. Yet God planned everything about you before you were even born. You may not know His reasons, but God does.

It hurts to be unpopular, especially when you are teased or insulted for some part of your appearance. You may wish you had what other people have. You might even try to become more like those people so that you are accepted. In some moments, you would give anything to be included.

Don't give up. God cares what you are going through, and He does not like it when you are treated badly – you are His kid! He is far more concerned with what is inside of you than what you have on the outside. Avoid falling into beauty traps, like going on dangerous diets. Instead, pray that God would show you the ways that He wants you to take care of your body and your heart.

Whenever you find yourself wishing for what others have – and maybe even wishing you were someone else altogether – picture yourself running to your Father. Follow Hannah's example: close your eyes and tell God everything that has happened. Then ask Him to show you how to overcome it. And He will.

TALKING WITH GOD

Father God, I am having a hard time liking who I am. I am tired of being teased. Sometimes I wish I could be somebody else. But I know that you made me, and you like me just as I am. Help me to see the things that you see in me, God. Show me how to accept what you've given me. I know that you care about me, and that you have good plans for me. Lord, please help me to forgive people who are mean. Change their hearts so that they care about other people's feelings. Amen.

MAKING CONNECTIONS

Girls are not the only ones who stress over their appearance. Guys often get the idea that when it comes to being a man, body-building means everything. But there are plenty of muscular athletes who are not very happy on the inside. Being a man is not defined by a body type — it is defined by the way you live your life.

Maybe the shoe is on the other foot for you; you have always been popular. Some people are blessed with good looks or an outgoing personality. If that's your story, thank God for giving you those things.

Hopefully you have not stepped on other people to become part of the 'in crowd.' Be honest — do you ever make fun of people? Maybe you do it because you want to look cooler than someone else. Or you may join in with others who tease the outcasts, just so you'll fit in.

Would you make fun of Jesus? You'd probably say "No." Yet each time you insult or exclude another person, you are actually doing it to Him. Ouch.

It's time to ask God to help you change direction. Be thankful for your blessings — but don't make them someone else's curse. God has given you gifts on the inside too. Ask Him to show you what those gifts are, and use them to be good to other people.

DIGGING DEEPER

"For You formed my inward parts; You covered me in my mother's womb. I will praise You, for I am fearfully and wonderfully made." *Ps. 139:13-14a.*

"...For he loved Hannah, although the LORD had closed her womb. And her rival also provoked her severely, to make her miserable, because the LORD had closed her womb." *1 Samuel 1: 5-6.*

"...You outwardly appear righteous to men, but inside you are full of hypocrisy and lawlessness."
Matthew 23:28.

I DIDN'T WANT TO MOVE

I hate this, Jess thought. He was supposed to be finished packing his room by now. Jess didn't even like packing to go away on vacation; now he was packing to go live in a new house.

Not that a new house was such a bad thing. Jess and Mom had lived in a noisy, cramped apartment for three years now – ever since Dad left. But the new house was in a different neighborhood — way too far from the skate park. How was he supposed to get there now? Jess would have to find a ride every time he wanted to go. He could just hear the guys now: *Hey, Jess — did your Mommy drive you today?*

As if that wasn't bad enough, now he'd have to go

to a totally different school. Jess had always thought he'd graduate at Jefferson High with all his friends – not to mention Maria Lopez. He had it bad for her.

It had taken him almost a year to ask Maria for help in Geometry. Now they were starting to talk about everyday stuff – not just math. And Maria had finally dumped her obnoxious boyfriend. So Jess was ready to make his move ... until he found out that he'd be forced to make a completely different kind of move.

Another thing about this move – it would not just be Jess and Mom in the new house. They were moving into Bob's house. Bob was Mom's boyfriend, and they were getting married in two weeks. Bob wore old-man shoes, and told stupid jokes. He also listened to the 'oldies' radio station.

Why couldn't Bob move to Mom's neighborhood instead? Jess thought angrily. The guy never even mentioned the move to Jess, or the marriage for that matter. It was like Bob couldn't care less what Jess thought about the whole thing.

Mom hadn't mentioned it either, until yesterday. She said something about not wanting to stress him out. *Yeah, great idea*, Jess thought sarcastically. *Just drop a bomb on me, Mom – no problem.*

Mom told him that they would stay at his uncle's

house until the wedding, because Uncle Ed lived close to Jefferson. Mom said this as if she was doing Jess some kind of a favor: "This way, you'll have time to say goodbye to your friends."

What good were a few more days? It wasn't going to change things; he would still have to leave.

He tried to explain this to Mom, but she just didn't get it.

"You'll meet new girls at Gruzer High," she said.

Gruzer?! Nice name. Rhymes with loser, thought Jess. *Which is basically what I'll be — the loser 'new kid' — thanks to Bob.*

Mom and Bob had no clue what a hassle it was for Jess to move. Especially without any notice! Was this how all decisions were going to be made from now on?

THINKING IT THROUGH

Moving to a new house is a huge change. It's the kind of decision that parents usually make *for* their kids, rather than *with* their kids – even if their kids are teens. This may seem really unfair to you. Like Jess, you may feel that your parents do not care about your feelings when a major decision is made.

In most cases it's not that your parents do not care how you feel. In fact, they probably care a lot about whether their choices will hurt your feelings. To avoid this, they may keep the truth from you until the last minute — like Jess's mom did. In the end, parents must decide what is best for the family as a group.

In families where the parents have never been divorced, the parents control the cash. So it kind of makes sense that money decisions are usually made by parents, not their kids. For example, a decision to move may happen for any number of reasons: a parent's new job, a need for more living space, a change to a better neighborhood, or even as a way to down size the bills. All of these reasons involve cash — parents' cash.

In the same way, the parents in a blended family[1] must also make money decisions. Once your parent decides to remarry, a new family is formed. Since the family members can't keep living in two separate places, your parent and stepparent must choose one of the two homes — or replace the two homes with a new one. Again it comes down to cash. Which parent makes more money? Can one parent change jobs, or relocate to a different office? Which place would make more sense, as far as traveling time? You may be thinking, *These things have nothing to do with my personal life.* It may seem like your parents care more

---

1. Blended family: a term used to describe a new family blended together from other family units, sometimes also described as stepfamily.

about their jobs or their new home than about you.

In spite of how things look right now, God cares very much about your personal life. He has a definite plan; just don't be surprised if it doesn't match yours! God sees your personal life much differently than you do. He sees the whole picture, not just what will happen next week. He often works through parents so that He can make the very best choices for their kids' lives.

In the Bible, there is a story of a teen named Daniel. He knew what it was like to be forced to move from his home. Daniel was a Jew, and his home was in a place called Judah. One day, the king of Babylon completely conquered Judah. To the Jews, it may have seemed as if God didn't care about them. But — check this out — the Bible tells us that God *allowed* Babylon to defeat the Jews. You see, God had a major plan.

Once Judah was defeated, Daniel and some of his friends were captured, and forced to live in Babylon. Then they had to complete three years of training to learn how to serve the king. The Babylonians even replaced the teens' names with pagan names.

Daniel and his friends were expected to learn and practice all the pagan customs. They would never be able to marry and have children. Nobody asked these guys whether or not they *wanted* to live this way; they were just told that they had to.

At the time, Daniel had no clue why God would let this happen to him. But the way he dealt with it was very cool. Instead of being angry at how his life was turning out, Daniel decided to trust God and obey His laws – no matter what was going on.

God rewarded Daniel for trusting Him. He gave Daniel the ability to interpret the king's dreams. The king was so pleased with this that he promoted Daniel and his three friends. Daniel got to sit in the official gate of the king. Eventually, God made Daniel a prophet in that kingdom.

God does understand that it is hard for us to accept change. We feel uneasy when we have no idea what the future will bring. Try your best to trust Him. Whenever you start to stress about the move, stop and say a quick prayer that God will help you deal with things. It may seem too simple – but it will work. Each time you ask for His help, your trust in Him will grow stronger.

It's also a good idea to talk to your parents. Be respectful, but honest. Explain that you are not happy with the move, and tell them why. If they have avoided telling you about the move until the last minute, you may want to talk about this too. Your purpose here is not to change their minds, but to help them understand the pressure you are under. This way, if you do blow up about something later, they'll probably be more understanding.

Before you move, you may want to ask your church or youth leader if they know of any churches in your new neighborhood. Having connections can help you plug in faster. If you are into sports or other activities, you could call recreation centers in the new neighborhood to find out what is offered there.

If you have to move to a new school, see if you can check it out ahead of time. Many schools have web sites with pictures and info. This will help you not to feel like an alien when you get there.

Speaking of the web, you might want to find out if there is a local teen chatroom for your town. You could end up 'meeting' some of the kids that go to your new school before you get there. Just remember to clear this with your parents before you do it.

Good things can happen because of this move. You may realize this right away, or you may not know the explanations for months. Either way, God is *allowing* this change. You're His kid, and He has a plan for you.

TALKING WITH GOD

Father God, I really want to trust You; but right now that's hard for me to do. I'm angry that I have to leave my friends behind. And right now, it seems like my parents don't care how I feel about it. Help me to get past that. Show me how to talk to my parents about my feelings. Thank You for the plan that You have for my life. Amen.

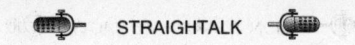

MAKING CONNECTIONS

Moves happen. Even if you've lived in the same house your whole life, there will be times when you are the new person. Starting high school or college is one example. It seems like everyone already knows exactly where to go — except you. Maybe you are trying out for a new sport. You can feel your new teammates sizing you up. Or you could be starting a new job. As if being the new person isn't tough enough, you also have to learn how to do new things. It can be very stressful to feel like everyone is staring at you, wondering who you are.

Remember that feeling the next time you are on the other side of the fence. When the new person shows up at your school, on your street or at church, make them feel welcome. Ask them something about themselves. Tell them a little about you. Show them how to navigate. This will show them that you care who they are — instead of just wondering what they are doing there.

I DIDN'T WANT TO MOVE

DIGGING DEEPER

"For I know the thoughts that I think toward you, says the LORD, thoughts of peace and not of evil, to give you a future and a hope," *Jeremiah 29:11*.

"Then the king promoted Daniel and gave him many great gifts; and he made him ruler over the whole province of Babylon...," *Daniel 2:48a*.

"Be of good courage, and He shall strengthen your heart, all you who hope in the LORD," *Psalm 31:24*.

PERSONAL SPACE? WHAT'S THAT?!

On Monday morning Sara's alarm clock did not ring. By some miracle she woke up on her own — half an hour later than usual. In a panic, she searched for a clean shirt — not an easy thing to find, thanks to her stepsister, Katie.

Last night it was Katie's turn to load the washer — but she 'forgot' to do Sara's laundry. *Just like she 'forgot' to wake me this morning*, Sara thought angrily. Katie knew that Sara had to get to school too!

Sara took a quick look in the bathroom mirror, and then wished she hadn't. There was an enormous zit on her chin. This was *not* a good sign of how the rest of the day would go. To make matters worse, her little stepbrother Troy was banging on the bathroom door. "I hafta *go!*" he whined.

Sara ran downstairs to grab a quick bowl of cereal before school. But of course, *somebody* had eaten the last of the cereal. *Somebody who never used to live here in the first place*, she thought. *Fine. I'll starve*. She rushed out the door to school.

School turned out to be another nightmare. There was a science test Sara had completely forgotten about, and a totally mean substitute teacher in math class. After a long walk home — it poured rain, of course – all she wanted was some personal space. Some *everyone-leave-me-alone* time.

She pushed open the front door and went straight upstairs to her room. Unfortunately, it was not just *her* room anymore – a fact which Sara still could not get used to. Katie was already there, painting her nails with three of her annoying friends. This was just too much to handle in one day.

"Get out of my room — *NOW!*" Sara yelled.

Katie glared back at Sara. "It's *my* room too," she announced. "Besides, I called Dad at work and he said it's OK for my friends to be here."

"He may be *your* dad, but he's not mine," Sara shot back.

PERSONAL SPACE? WHAT'S THAT?!

She slammed the door and went downstairs.

No personal space there, either. In the living-room, Troy was watching an annoying little kid movie with a singing lizard.

How lame, Sara thought. She couldn't even chill out in the kitchen. Mom was there, completely absorbed in preparing her new husband's favorite meal – pot roast. *Totally gross*.

Sara was angry, and there was no place she could go. So she picked a fight with Troy. "Little *babies* watch lizard movies!" she shouted, as she stood in front of the TV to block his view. Troy burst into tears. Mom rushed in to save him. "Sara! Be nice to your little brother."

Now Sara felt tears on her own cheeks. "Mom! He is *not* my brother!!! This used to be *our* house – just you and me. Why couldn't things just stay that way?"

Sara's stepsister and her friends were watching the whole thing from the stairs, smirking. *This is a joke!* Sara thought. *Will I ever have breathing room again?*

THINKING IT THROUGH

It can be frustrating if new people move into your house, or if you have to move into someone else's home. Either way, there is definitely less breathing room for everyone involved. You have instant family members, whether you wanted them or not. It's one thing to adjust to a new stepparent; but when you throw in new stepbrothers or stepsisters things can get crazy — especially when it comes to sharing a room.

Before your living situation changed you may have made most of the decisions about your room: how it was decorated, when you would use it, where things were kept. Not any more. Now there may be one, or even two other kids with whom you have to share it.

Like Sara, you may feel forced into a living situation which you did not ask for. Adjusting is not easy for anyone in this situation. It is natural for us to want time to ourselves. God knows how frustrated you feel. His own Son was part of a *stepfamily*.

Jesus had a stepfather, at least four half-brothers, and two half-sisters. He probably struggled for privacy, just as you do. Even when He was older, Jesus had a hard time finding space — He often went far off into the wilderness, just so that He could be alone and pray.

Because of the pressures of school, friends and your future, sometimes it's hard to feel calm and peaceful. And your new family situation just adds to your stress. So what can you do?

First, you can pray each morning for Jesus to give you peace. The Bible tells us that Jesus is the Prince of

PERSONAL SPACE? WHAT'S THAT?!

Peace. He can give us a peace that is more powerful than any peaceful moment we might have on our own. It is not the kind of peace that lasts for a few minutes; instead, it is something that changes us on the inside, so that even our rough times don't seem nearly as bad.

Are you at peace with God? That can only happen once you truly give your life to His Son, Jesus. Giving your life to Him means that you want to follow Him, obey Him and trust Him with each day of your life. Jesus has forgiven you for everything you've done in the past. He died for you because He loves you that much.

Once you know and follow Jesus, you can begin to have real peace. Take a few minutes each morning to ask Jesus for peace. You will find that no matter what your day is like, Jesus is right there with you. He helps you deal with things in a calmer way.

Next make a plan to have some privacy. Talk with your stepbrother or stepsister about working out a schedule for the room. If you are not able to talk things out peacefully, ask your parents to hold a family meeting. This will give everyone a chance to have their say – with your parents there to referee, in case anyone is not fair.

Try taking up walking or running twice a week. Exercise is a good way to work off anger or frustration, and it also gives you time to think and pray. You will soon feel better on the inside *and* on the outside.

Adjustment to your new living situation will take time. The most important thing you can do right now is ask Jesus for His peace. Once your soul has breathing room, the rest will follow.

TALKING WITH GOD

Lord Jesus, You know what it's like to be a teenager in a crowded house. It's hard for me to share my home – especially my room – with my new family. Please fill my heart with your peace. Help me to stay calm when I feel crowded, and show me some ways that I can have some privacy. Amen.

MAKING CONNECTIONS

Do you have a friend with a major space shortage? Help them gain some space. Offer to help rearrange their room, put up shelves or paint the walls so that the space feels comfortable – even if it's tight. If your space is larger, share it. Invite your friend over for dinner one night a week. Do homework together in peace and quiet at your house.

You could also meet your friend at a library to do homework. Or you can go to a park to shoot hoops or talk. Become workout partners at the gym. Trade prayer requests once a week about your space issues, or anything else that is stressing you. In a strange way, a lack of space is a blessing – it helps you to think creatively!

DIGGING DEEPER

"And the peace of God, which surpasses all understanding, will guard your hearts and minds through Christ Jesus," *Philippians 4:7*.

"Peace I leave with you. My peace I give to you; not as the world gives do I give to you. Let not your heart be troubled, neither let it be afraid," *John 14:27*.

"...As much as depends on you, live peaceably with all men," *Romans 12:18*.

NO TIME FOR GOD

"Sean! LET'S GO!" Dad shouted up the stairs for the third time.

Sean was not into the idea of church today. He didn't sleep well last night. He had two tests coming up, and he still needed to study. Most importantly, he had to call his girlfriend, Shannon. He decided that church would have to wait until next week; one week off never hurt anybody.

"I can't go today," Sean called down the stairs.

Dad came up the stairs to Sean's door with an aggravated look on his face. "Mom is waiting in the car with your sisters. You are holding us up. What's the deal?"

"I can't go, Dad. I think I'm getting a cold."

Sean felt bad about the lie. But he pushed the guilt out of his mind.

"Alright. Maybe just this once you should go back to bed. Do you need anything?" asked Dad.

"No, I should be fine," he answered, sniffling.

"OK, see you when we get back," said Dad.

As his father walked out the door, Sean felt relieved. It wasn't that he didn't like church. But these days, Sean was having a hard time squeezing God into his schedule.

He used to read his Bible before school each day. But since he started dating Shannon, he stayed up late talking to her on the phone. When morning came, he usually hit the snooze button.

Sean hadn't seen his friends at Wednesday night youth group very much lately either. Wednesday was Shannon's night off from work. Sean wanted to keep her happy, so he hung out with her instead. Besides, Shannon wasn't into the whole 'church thing.'

It had taken Sean a long time to ask Shannon out. He figured she'd turn him down. She was a cheerleader, and all of the guys at school liked her. But now Shannon was his girlfriend. His girlfriend! How did that happen?! Everyone was jealous.

Still ... something wasn't right.

What's wrong with me? Sean asked himself. I finally score a chance with Shannon, and I'm not happy.

Pushing his doubt aside, he called his girlfriend. Sean noticed that Shannon spent a lot of time talking about herself. When she wasn't doing that, she was complaining about other people.

Sean's mind started to drift. He found himself wishing he hadn't lied to his parents. He actually missed being at church. Even when he reminded himself that he was talking to the best-looking girl at school, Sean felt empty.

THINKING IT THROUGH

Schedules can create pressure. Certain events can't be moved around to different time slots - like school or work. Other activities may have more flexible time slots, but they still need to be done - like studying or chores.

Then there are the fun things on the list - the things we do just because we want to. Most of these activities can be postponed. Strangely enough, those are the things we stubbornly keep on the day planner!

Many of us forget that God should be the top priority. Do you find yourself passing over prayer time because you are running late? You may reason that God wants you to finish certain things on your schedule, so He will understand. At other times, you may skip going to church to do something that you think is more fun ... everybody needs to have down-time, don't they? Or maybe you neglect time with God unintentionally – you find that you always forget to read your Bible.

Focusing on a relationship with God is not always an easy thing to do, especially when you are trying to balance school, work and a social life. It is not wrong to have fun. We all need down-time now and then. Even Jesus, the busiest guy who ever lived, pencilled in some relaxation – although he was usually interrupted! But there was one major difference. Jesus' main focus was God.

Jesus is human as well as Divine. On earth He enjoyed fun just as much as the next person. He liked being with friends – talking, eating and just chilling. But He never did those things until He had taken care of the things that God wanted Him to do. Even in His down-time He was praying, or sharing the word of God.

Sean's relationship with Shannon was nothing like that. Rather than filling his mind with the words of the Bible, he was listening to Shannon's gossip. Instead of spending time with friends who were learning about God, he was spending time with someone who chose not to have God in her life. As a result he was starting to lie, and ditch his responsibilities.

You may not have realized this, but if your relationship

with God is not the most important thing on your schedule, then you are breaking one of the Ten Commandments. God told Moses that it is wrong for people to make anything in their lives more important than their relationship with Him.

Sean began to feel empty when he crossed out God and penciled in Shannon. At first he felt happy. But he knew in his heart that dating Shannon was causing him to ignore school, family, friends and God. Like Sean, even if you cross out God in your day planner, you will not be able to replace Him. The things you enjoy doing most will lose their meaning when you leave God out of the picture. But if you put Him first, you will find that all the other things on your schedule will fall into place.

Ask yourself some important questions:

• Are you focusing on people or things more than your relationship with God?

• Who are your friends, and what do you talk about with them?

• Do these people care about God?

• Picture Jesus sitting with you during your free time. Would He be proud of you?

Don't worry if your answers tell you that you are not focusing on God, you can change this! Start by setting a daily slot in your schedule for prayer. The earlier, the better – talking with God gives you a peace to carry through your whole day, even when things get crazy.

Maybe you are worried that if you set a prayer time slot, you will be late for other things. Make a choice to trust God. He knows every event on your schedule. As you pray each morning, ask Him to show you how He wants your checklist to look — including your down-time. He will show you what is really important. You may be surprised to find that if you do things God's way, juggling your schedule is not nearly as stressful!

Finally, trust God to bring good people into your life, whether they are friends or dating relationships. Anyone who separates you from your relationship with God is eventually going to bring you trouble. If you feel that God is telling you this about a certain person, listen to Him. He wants what is best for you.

Some of your relationships will have to change. You may have to let go of other friends altogether. It will be hard to let these relationships go. Yet if you focus on giving God top priority in your life, you will handle disappointments and losses much better.

TALKING WITH GOD

Dear God, I am not putting you first in my schedule. I know that I should, but sometimes I have trouble remembering or believing that. Show me if there are any people or things in my life that are hurting my relationship with You. If there are, then please give me the courage to change things. Amen.

THINKING IT THROUGH

Unlike Sean, you may be on track with God right now. Great! Then you know what a difference it makes when He is a big part of your day.

There are times when it seems easier to stay tuned in to God. Make the most of times like that to prepare yourself for rough days in the future. You may not want to think about it, but hard times will come – life is like that! So now is the time to fine-tune your agenda.

While things are low-key, consider keeping a journal to check your progress. Here are some questions you may consider answering every few days:
- What important verses jumped out at me?
- Did God tell me something during prayer time?
- Has He answered a specific prayer?

If you are not into writing, choose a close friend and share your answers with them. Or maybe you could e-mail your youth pastor once in awhile. You will be surprised at how this helps you stay focused on God. It may help your friends to tune in too!

DIGGING DEEPER

"You shall have no other gods before Me," *Exodus 20:3*.

"Observe and obey all these words which I command you, that it may go well with you ... forever, when you do what is good and right in the sight of the LORD your God," *Deuteronomy 12:28*.

"But He was in the stern, asleep on a pillow. And they awoke Him..." *Mark 4:38a*.

THAT USED TO BE MY JOB!

Bethany was so tired of her stepmom squeezing in on her turf. What right did she have to just move in and take over? Bethany – along with her younger sister, Megan, and her dad – had been doing just fine for three years, thank you very much.

When Bethany's parents divorced, Mom left Dad to go live with her boyfriend. *What a good example*, Bethany thought bitterly. At the time, Dad fell apart; he just sat around looking sad. Dad needed someone to take care of him. So Bethany promised herself that she would do it, just the way Mom was *supposed to.*

From that point on, Bethany took over all of the things that Mom would have done. She cooked dinner, did the laundry and cleaned up after Dad. She even got on Megan's case if chores or homework weren't done, just like Mom used to do. She packed Dad's lunch, and asked him about his day when he got home from work.

As time passed, Dad slowly came around. He wasn't what Bethany would call 'happy', but at least he was smiling once in awhile. And Bethany felt good about helping him. Then came Ann.

Once Dad started dating Ann, life was different. At first, things seemed to change for the better. Dad finally seemed happy. He was actually shopping for clothes!

Bethany helped him pick out stuff so he'd look cool and a little less 'Dad'. He asked Bethany for advice about places to take Ann, gifts to buy her, etc.

Ann was really nice too. She was easy to talk to. Soon Bethany began calling Ann after school, just to chat about her day. It was nice to have a female adult to turn to, especially since Mom was not so great at listening these days.

One day, Dad told Bethany that he would ask Ann to marry him. He took Bethany with him to pick out the ring. He even followed Bethany's advice about how and when to propose to Ann.

Once Dad and Ann were engaged, Ann asked Bethany to be her Maid of Honor. Bethany helped Dad and Ann with decisions about the wedding details. Ann bought Bethany an awesome dress, too.

The wedding day was a lot of fun. But once Dad and Ann left for their honeymoon, Bethany started to feel worried. Even a little jealous ... OK, a lot jealous. But she wasn't sure why.

She tried to talk herself out of it. *It's not like Dad is my boyfriend or anything*, she reasoned. *So why should I be jealous?* It really bugged her to feel that way.

She called Dad's cell phone a few times. He never even answered it; he'd probably turned it off. She didn't leave a message the first few times.

Bethany and Megan were staying at Pastor Johnson's house, and Dad had told the pastor's wife to call the hotel if there was any kind of emergency. Nothing was really an emergency right now, but still...

She asked Mrs. Johnson for the number to the hotel, but she wouldn't give it to Bethany. She said that newlyweds need their privacy. So Bethany decided to leave a few messages on Dad's cell phone, just to let him know how she felt about the whole thing:

"Dad - what's the deal? Just because you're on your honeymoon doesn't give you the right to blow us off."

"Dad - when are you coming home? Are you even listening to your messages?!"

STRAIGHTTALK

Finally, the honeymoon ended. Now Bethany had a completely different opinion of Ann. After all, Ann was the one who had caused Dad to ignore his own children.

By Monday, Bethany's whole world had turned upside-down. Before Ann moved in, Bethany had always done whatever she pleased until Dad got home. She liked having that freedom. But that Monday, Ann was already there when Bethany arrived home from school.

Feeling irritated, Bethany decided to go out and get the mail for Dad. At least she could open all the junk letters for him like she usually did. But the mailbox was empty because Ann had already done it.

By then, Bethany was really starting to feel annoyed. She went into the kitchen to cook some dinner for Dad. But of course, Ann was already there — cooking a gourmet dinner which was way more complicated than anything Bethany had ever made.

But the worst part was when Dad walked in the door. He used to say hi to Bethany and Megan, then sit down next to Bethany and talk about his day. Not anymore. Now he looked for his wife. He went right over to Ann and kissed her *first*. For some strange reason, Megan didn't even seem to mind. But it really made Bethany angry. As if that wasn't enough, Dad went into another room with Ann – *to talk about his day!*

Bethany wished that Dad had never married Ann. *After all I did to help him through his bad times*, thought Bethany, *now he acts like it meant nothing to him*. She fought back tears of anger. Bethany felt like she was no longer needed.

THINKING IT THROUGH

Why is it sometimes so hard to watch someone else find happiness? At one time or another, it has probably happened to you; maybe it is going on in your life right now. Someone you love very much has been struggling through a major hard time – and you have been there for that person all along, running for the tissue box. You were definitely, critically, unquestionably needed. Eventually that person begins to see a light at the end of the tunnel. They start to live a little, and soon they are even smiling and laughing again. And then something, or maybe some*one*, happens to them. Suddenly they seem to have peace, success and joy. Which is just what you wanted for them all along ... isn't it?

Except why is it that you feel so unappreciated? So unimportant? So *resentful*?

This type of situation often happens to teens if their parents divorce, or if a parent dies. If you have a good relationship with your parents, then of course you don't like to see them hurting. It's bad enough that you've got your own heartache going on. But seeing your parents with broken hearts can make you crazy.

There is usually one child in the family who feels responsible to hold things together while a parent is hurting, just as Bethany did. Many times, it is the oldest child who takes on this role; or it might be the child who is the same gender as the parent who left. For example, if a father leaves, then his son might step up to protect the mother and the rest of the family.

You may be taking on extra chores around the house, running errands and doing many other things which used to be handled by the 'missing' parent. You may even begin to notice that the conversations you have with your live-in parent have become more involved. Lately you are talking with them about their job, their money concerns, and even issues concerning your brothers or sisters — in the same way that your parents used to discuss things together.

You may feel that you like this new role. After all, now you are a part of the solution. It keeps you busy and makes you feel useful. It takes your mind off of your own issues. After awhile, it's as if you're on a mission: *I will get my parent through this.* It is almost like you are no longer a kid; you actually begin to feel like you are your parent's peer.

MAJOR RED FLAG! No matter how much you love your parent, you've got to put the brakes on here.

You may be familiar with the story of Creation. But did you ever take a good look at how it applies to families? Here's the deal: When God created Adam, He noticed that Adam was lonely. So God decided to make a companion for Adam - someone who would be his friend, his helper and his love.

The Bible tells us that these two companions were to be so close that they were like one flesh. They would become two parts that make up one whole - kind of like when you roll together two pieces of clay, and then you can't see where one stops and the other starts.

Notice that God did not make a son or a daughter to fill this place in Adam's life. God gave Adam a wife.

There is no type of human-to-human relationship that should be as intimate as the one between a husband and wife. This is not just God's 'suggestion'. It is His law. This means that except for a person's own relationship with God, there should be no other relationship in a family which is placed above the husband and the wife's relationship. When the marriage relationship is the top priority, then the whole family will be blessed - because every other type of relationship in that family will be stronger as a result.

You may be thinking, *OK, fine ... but it didn't turn out that way for MY family*. That's a good point. If your parents have divorced, then God's perfect plan was not followed. If one parent has died, then the other parent has great struggles. Death was never part of God's perfect plan for this world – sin made it that way. So whenever God's perfect plan is not in place, the family struggles. This is why your family is dealing with some very painful issues right now.

You have tried to help your hurting parent fill in that big hole in your family so your heart is in the right place. In your own mind, your solution may seem to be the easiest way to make things better. So you begin to move in fast-forward, without checking to see if your plan matches up with God's.

God really appreciates your kindness toward your parent during this time. He will truly bless you for your desire to help. The Bible tells us that it is good for children to take care of their parents.

Yet in the end, God does not want you playing a role that is not meant to be yours. He has given your parent a new companion. What a blessing! That person will now become one flesh with your parent, so that God's plan can again be restored in your family. And that will mean good things for everyone involved.

When it comes down to it, this is not really an issue between you and your parent. It is not even an issue between you and your new stepparent. In the end, it is an issue between you and God.

Sometimes it is hard to give God control. You have invested a lot of time, energy and tears into playing this role of 'guardian angel'. It has become a habit, and habits can be hard to break. Where do you start?

Begin by praying that God will help you to have peace about your stepparent's new position in the family. This will not come naturally! God understands that; after all, you're only human. So ask for His help.

As you pray, try making a list of the things that you now have more time to do. It's kind of nice not to have so much extra work to do, isn't it? Use that list to thank God for the spare time He has given you.

Speaking of spare time, why spend it feeling angry or jealous? Why not use it to try something new? Is there a sport you've wanted to try? An after-school activity? Could you make some extra money babysitting? Is there some place you could volunteer after school?

It would also be very helpful to have a heart-to-heart with your stepparent. Chances are, your stepparent is not aware that you are feeling hurt. Do not assume that they don't care about your feelings; it is more likely that they don't know you well enough yet.

Since they do not yet know you as well as your parent does, it may take them a bit longer to notice that there is a problem. Remember, they are only human too. Before the two of you sit down to talk, ask God to help you express your feelings clearly and kindly.

When it comes to life plans, you will never be able to outdo God. He loves you dearly, and knows what is best for you. He made you into the person you are.

Right now you are a teen, which is just the way God wants things. Enjoy it. Take off your 'serious adult' shoes, and pass them over to your stepparent. You've got some living to do!

TALKING WITH GOD

Dear Lord, I'm thankful that my parent has found someone to love, but sometimes I feel like I'm not important anymore. I feel resentful toward my new stepparent. Show me how to deal with this in a better way. Remind me how much my parent has always loved me, and help me to trust that I will continue to be loved just as much. Please help me to learn what a true marriage should be, so that some day I can bless my own family. Amen.

MAKING CONNECTIONS

Help a friend adjust to a new stepfamily situation. It may be hard for your friend to see objectively right now; they can only see how they have been hurt. It is important to let your friend share their feelings when necessary. But also, encourage them to see the issue from the other perspective. Like any problem in life, the people involved may be looking at the issue from very different angles. Help your friend remember to relax. It must have been a rough ride filling in for their other parent. They need your encouragement. Invite them to leave their stress behind for a while and have fun.

DIGGING DEEPER

"And the LORD God said, It is not good that man should be alone; I will make him a helper comparable to him," *Genesis 2:18*.

"Then the rib which the LORD God had taken from man He made into a woman, and He brought her to the man. And Adam said: This is now bone of my bones and flesh of my flesh; she shall be called Woman, because she was taken out of Man," *Genesis 2:22-23*.

"Therefore a man shall leave his father and mother and be joined to his wife, and they shall become one flesh," *Genesis 2:24*.

BUT HE'S NOT MY REAL FATHER

It was Friday afternoon. Miguel decided to go to his friend Sam's house after school. He wasn't in a hurry to get home. On Fridays his stepfather, Carlos, worked at home. Miguel was in no mood to play 'Twenty Questions'. Carlos liked to grill Miguel about what he did, where he went, who he talked to ... it was crazy. Mom said that Carlos was only trying to get to know him better. Miguel wasn't so sure about that.

Sam had a serious collection of video games. And – even better – Sam's parents were still at work when he got home from school every day.

Miguel was just about to reach the next level in Sam's new game.

"You've got *skills*!" Sam yelled. Then the phone rang.

"It's your stepdad," said Sam, passing the phone to Miguel. "How did he even know you were *here*?"

Miguel made a face. "Who knows?" he asked, reaching for the phone. "He needs to get a life."

Miguel made it clear to Carlos that he was annoyed. "Well, what do you want?"

"Miguel, *where are you?!* It's *4:30.*"

"You already know where I am. You called *me*," Miguel answered rudely.

Carlos was angry. "Well, I shouldn't have to call around to find out where you are."

"I agree," said Miguel. "It's none of your business where I am."

"It certainly *is* my business," said Carlos firmly. "You have no right to be wandering around after school without telling anyone where you are."

Miguel felt his temperature rising. "Why? It's not like I'm out dealin' drugs to little kids."

"Because I said so, that's why," Carlos demanded. "And by the way, if you have any homework you need to finish it before you do anything else this weekend."

"Since when? Who are you, the Homework Police?" Miguel shot back. "You're not my father. You never will be. So stop trying to tell me what to do."

Carlos was furious. "No, I'm not your father. But I *am* your stepdad. And I've had about enough of your backtalk. So get home. NOW."

"What*ever!*" Miguel yelled as he slammed the phone down. He felt like punching a wall.

Sam looked concerned. "What was *that* about?"

"My stepfather has control issues," Miguel said. "I gotta go."

As he left Sam's house Miguel thought, *Maybe I'll just go somewhere else. Who is he to tell me to come home?*

Just one problem with that idea — Mom would worry when she found out that Miguel hadn't returned. And she would definitely find out. Carlos would call her at work and tell her, for sure. Instead, he decided to walk home and get it over with.

When Miguel reached the front door his stepfather was already standing there with a big scowl on his face. *Carlos is ready to rumble*, Miguel thought sarcastically.

"Miguel ...," his stepdad began in a no-nonsense tone.

Miguel cut him off. "I can't believe you actually called around looking for me! Do you have any idea how embarrassing that is?!"

"Well, who's fault is that?" Carlos replied. "If you had

asked me if you could go to Sam's, then I wouldn't need to check up on you."

"Of course you wouldn't — because I wouldn't have been allowed out in the first place!" Miguel shouted.

Carlos was losing his cool; his face resembled a pit-bull.

"Look, Miguel – you are a teenager, not an adult. Some day you will be able to come and go as you please. But right now, you are not in charge!"

Miguel responded by grabbing the remote and turning on the TV, cranking the volume as loud as he could.

Carlos grabbed the remote out of Miguel's hand. "When I draw a line, you do not cross it. No, I am not your father; but I am an adult, and you need to respect that. *Do you understand?*"

Deep down, Miguel knew that the way he was acting was not cool. He never talked to Mom the way he was talking to Carlos right now. But Miguel could not seem to stop himself from standing his ground.

"And if I cross the line, what are you gonna do about it?" he asked, glaring at Carlos.

Carlos was done arguing. "Miguel," he said simply, "you are grounded for the weekend. No TV, no phone, no friends."

Miguel got in one last jab. "You may be an adult, but

that doesn't give you the right to be a jerk."

Miguel's timing couldn't have been worse. There was Mom, standing in the doorway with tears in her eyes. "Miguel Rodriguez," she said quietly, "you will not speak to my husband that way. It dishonors me, as well as Carlos."

The hurt look in his mother's eyes was far worse than being grounded. Miguel hated to disappoint her. His real father had given her enough sadness for a lifetime.

"Mom ..." Miguel started to say.

But Mom did not want to discuss it. "No more words, Miguel. Get to your room."

As he climbed the stairs, Miguel's heart felt heavy. *How did this happen?* he wondered. *Do I really have to answer to Carlos from now on?* Miguel's eighteenth birthday was two years away. It seemed like a hundred.

THINKING IT THROUGH

You get into a certain pattern in life, and it works for you. Then something or someone comes along to change the rules. Your first instinct is to protest.

Sometimes it is good to resist change. Not all changes are necessary, and some can even be harmful. Just like the saying goes: *If it ain't broke, don't fix it.*

Many times, the reason that people do not like change

is because they don't want to leave their comfort zone. Others just like to argue; if they didn't get to vote on an idea, they automatically oppose it.

Living in a one-parent home can sometimes be low-maintenance, as far as expectations go. With only one parent to make the decisions in your home, you don't need to wait for them to talk things over with another adult before giving you an answer. Before Carlos became Miguel's stepfather, his mother was the only decision-maker in the home.

Single parents work really hard to take care of their families. They are actually doing the work of two parents. Many times they are exhausted. When single parents are feeling overloaded, sometimes rules and consequences are not enforced.

But when a single parent gets married, everything changes. Suddenly there are two people making the rules. Sometimes the rules change completely, as they did in Miguel's house when his mother married Carlos.

You may be experiencing the same frustrations with your new stepparent. Who is this new person to just walk into your family and expect you to obey?! Can they really do that?

While there are plenty of clear-cut guidelines in the Bible about respecting your parents, there are no specific

BUT HE'S NOT MY REAL FATHER

commandments about stepparents. So does this mean that you're off the hook?

Not exactly. While there are no rules specifically about respecting stepparents, the Bible does give examples of children who were raised by people *other than their parents*. The children were expected to obey that adult.

Samuel, for example, lived with his parents until he was about three years old. Then he went to live with Eli, a Jewish priest. Although Samuel's parents were still alive, it was Eli to whom he had to answer to each day. Samuel eventually grew up to be a great man of God.

Esther, a Jewish teenager, was raised by an older cousin named Mordecai. At that time, the king of Persia was looking for a new wife. Every teenage girl in the area was commanded to enter a competition to become his wife. Esther won the contest and became the queen.

Meanwhile, Mordecai found out that two of the king's men wanted to kill all the Jews. Mordecai told Esther to convince the king to spare her people. But at that time if you approached the king without being asked, the punishment was death! Esther knew that Mordecai was asking her to do something that could end her life.

Even though Esther was really scared, she obeyed Mordecai. And God blessed her! The king did not punish her for approaching him. Instead, he granted her request to spare the Jews.

Stepparents may not be birth parents. But it is God who has brought them to your family, to fill the empty hole where a parent should be. God expects a stepfather to be the *family* leader. The family *leader* is the one who makes the final decisions in the home, for the wife as well as the kids.

In the same way, God wants a stepmother to *watch over* the things that go on in the home, just as a birth-mother would if she lived there instead. Being a stepparent does not exclude a woman from being the family care-taker.

Since your stepparents are carrying out these God-given roles, then you must obey them just as you would obey your birth parents. It is understandable that you might be confused by the changes in your family. God knows that you are struggling to make sense of everything, and He cares about you very much. But resisting the change will only make things more difficult.

On the other hand, it is certainly OK to talk with your parent and stepparent about your feelings and ideas. It will help them to understand things from your side. Maybe you will be able to understand things from their side too.

However, there will still be days when you feel that your stepparent's decisions are unfair. This makes it even harder to obey them. But remember, God is your Father above anyone else. You must answer to Him. How do you think He would want you to respond to your stepparent? When you look at it from that perspective, the rest falls into place.

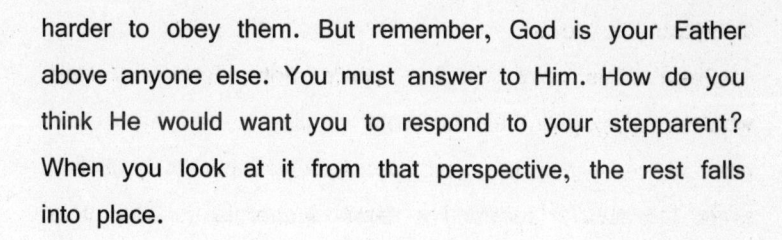

TALKING WITH GOD

Father God, It's hard for me to obey my stepparent. I haven't known this person all my life, the way I've known my real parent. I know that You want me to respect adults, even when I don't agree with them. Give me the strength to accept my stepparent's direction. Amen.

MAKING CONNECTIONS

How is the line drawn? When do you stop being treated like a kid, and start being treated more like an adult? And why don't all homes decide this the same way?

Maybe you have friends who are never allowed to do anything, whether it's against God's rules are not. Their parents seem to shelter them from every possible bad influence. Whether you are the teen under house arrest, or the friend looking in – it may not seem fair. At times, it may seem ridiculous. But the good news is that you are getting a chance to learn valuable stuff about being an adult. If you or your friend cannot do something, look up what God says about it. Journal it. If He says it's wrong, write down the reasons why, and the verses that gave you the answer. Then accept it. This will give you good practice for listening to bosses, professors and other supervisors as an adult. If God says that it is OK for you or your friend to do something, journal that too. Then, ask God to help you calmly and respectfully present your view to your parents. This will be great practice for negotiating as an adult.

DIGGING DEEPER

"Therefore, just as the church is subject to Christ, so let the wives be to their own husbands in everything," *Ephesians 5:24*.

"(A wife) watches over the ways of her household, and does not eat the bread of idleness," *Proverbs 31:27*.

"Children, obey your parents in all things, for this is well pleasing to the Lord," *Colossians 3:20*.

WHY WAIT?

It was finally Friday. Doreen couldn't wait to see Jared. On the weekends she got to spend much more time with him. Things seemed to be getting more serious between them. Last weekend, Jared told Doreen that he liked her more than any girl he'd ever been with.

Usually Doreen and Jared met up with their friends to see a movie at the mall, but tonight Jared picked her up in his brother's car and they drove to the movies – alone.

Dad would flip out if he knew, she thought as she said a quick goodbye and hurried out the door. In the dark movie theater, Doreen felt a rush of excitement. Jared steered her towards the back row. He held Doreen's hand as they sat down. When the movie started, he leaned toward her ear.

"Umm ... I think I love you," Jared said nervously.

Doreen almost fell out of her seat. She felt her whole face turning red. She tried to talk, but her tongue felt like it was made of brick. Jared waited anxiously for her to respond.

OK, now is not a good time to freak out, she scolded herself. "I love you too," she finally managed to say.

"Cool," said Jared, looking relieved.

Then he kissed her. Except this kiss was different than normal. This time, he didn't stop.

Doreen felt nervous, but she just went with it. Jared loved her, didn't he? He was just showing her how much. She told herself that a long kiss is probably OK if you love someone.

Except that's not where it stopped, either. Now Jared was rubbing his hands on her back. Doreen had a feeling that he wasn't planning to end the kiss any time soon. In a way she was glad, because kissing Jared felt good. She wondered how far things would go.

But Doreen knew it was wrong to be thinking that way. Mom had shown her all the places in the Bible where God said to wait to have sex. She had explained that sex was a gift from God, a present that was only meant to be opened by Doreen's husband on their wedding night.

So why do I want to forget all of that right now? she asked herself, moving closer to Jared.

Doreen reasoned that it was OK to fool around with Jared. *You never know, I might marry him someday. Besides, technically I'm not actually having sex ... yet. Although I bet that would be awesome*, she thought.

Doreen looked at the 'promise ring' her father had given her on her 12th birthday. She remembered him explaining how important it was to have self-control with boys, so that she could save herself for her husband one day. Dad also told Doreen that if a guy truly loves God – and her – then he will want to wait too.

Does this mean Jared doesn't really love God? Or me?

Doreen felt Jared pulling her closer. She was having trouble keeping her thoughts clear. She had no idea what to do.

THINKING IT THROUGH

You finally find a great person. There is serious chemistry between the two of you. The closer you get, the closer you want to get. It seems only natural that if you are close emotionally, you should be close physically too. If it seems so natural, then why is it wrong?

True, it is natural to want intimacy with a person of the opposite sex, especially once you become very close to that person. God created us so that we would have dreams and emotions. He gives us the ability to have desires, including sexual ones. Sex itself is not a sin; physical intimacy between a guy and a girl is one of the coolest gifts that God gave humans. But premarital sex has always been a sin in God's eyes. It is an issue of timing: ours versus His.

Like all gifts God has given us, sex has a purpose — His purpose, not ours. God created marriage when he made Adam and Eve. God wanted them to be completely intimate with each other in every way. Sexual intimacy creates a deep, loving bond. Marriage is meant to be the strongest relationship that a man and a woman could ever have, and sex is a beautiful way to express such a deep love. Sex is meant to be a promise that two people will be together for life.

God also created sexual intimacy so that humans could have children. Ever since He created the first couple on earth, God's will has been that sex and pregnancy happen only within marriage. Children were meant to learn how to have a loving marriage from their parents' example. So many children today do not have this, and God is sad for them.

In our confused world, there are many parents who have never been married at all; and there are even families with same-sex parents. Even if these couples really seem to love each other, remember – God tells us that *any* sex outside of a marriage between one man and one woman is wrong. Homosexuality is wrong because it is against God's law, and goes against His created plan for sex. Marriage is a gift from God to men and women.

Like Doreen, even if you know the reasons that God wants people to save sex for marriage, you may have trouble waiting. When you really care about someone, it is easy to get carried away by your emotions. You may wonder why God would give you strong desires for things that he does not want you to do.

Did you know that young people in the Bible have gone through this too? When Jacob met Rachel, he had a huge crush on her. Rachel's father told Jacob that he had to wait seven years before he was allowed to marry Rachel. The Bible doesn't tell us much about how Jacob was feeling ... but can't you just imagine? As much as he loved Rachel, Jacob probably wished his wedding night would get there already!

God is telling you to wait because He is protecting you. He wants you to have the gift of sexual intimacy, but He wants you to trust Him that it will be worth the wait. God has the right person picked out for you – and it may not be the person you've chosen for yourself. Even if the one you're with is a great person — that person may not be the best match for you.

Just think how cool it would be if you waited for that special person whom God picked, just for you. But how do you wait? Sexual purity takes self-control, and this starts in the mind. All people are tempted to sin. Our minds decide whether or not we will carry out those sins. Doreen knew in her mind that she and Jared should not be physically intimate. She thought of the things her parents had taught her — things that God says in the Bible.

At that point, Doreen had a choice. She could focus on what she wanted, and push God out of her mind, or she could focus on what God wanted, and push the temptation out of her mind. That is the secret to overcoming temptation.

When a thought about sex is in your mind, choose right away not to take that thought any further. It may be fun, but you have to trust God — He knows that it's not the right time in your life to have that kind of fun.

If someone really loves you the way God wants him or her to, they will not tempt you to have sex before marriage. If you can't see eye to eye about this, don't ignore it. Even though it will hurt to lose this person, it may be time to re-think the relationship.

Scripture does give us some good news about temptation.

First, God is faithful to those who stay close to Him. He promises that you will never be tempted beyond what you can handle. Second, there will always be a way to escape the temptation. You just need to make sure that you are always looking for the exit door.

One more thing about sex: Trust God. The more you count on Him, the stronger you will become.

TALKING WITH GOD

Dear Lord, sometimes I wonder what it would be like to have sex. I see it all around me – on TV, in the movies and in the magazines I read. Lots of kids at school believe that it's no big thing to have sex outside of marriage.

Sometimes I just want to give in, like everyone else. It's hard to be different from the rest of the world. Help me to save myself for the person that you have for me. I need self-control, Lord. Please show me a way out whenever I am tempted. Amen.

MAKING CONNECTIONS

Even if you are not in a relationship right now, you should prepare your mind and heart for a time when you may start dating. The stronger your relationship with God, the easier it will be to hear Him – even when you are tempted to do what is wrong. You may have a friend right now who is serious about someone, and thinking about having sex. Be there to listen. Everyone needs to share true feelings — even people who love God. We are all human. Remind your friend of how great it would be to wait. You can be like the friends of Solomon's girlfriend: show that you care and help to keep your friend strong. The more support you give, the more likely your friend will be to stay on the right track.

DIGGING DEEPER

"So Jacob served seven years for Rachel, and they seemed only a few days to him because of the love he had for her," *Genesis 29:20*.

"Do not stir up nor awaken love until it pleases," *Song of Songs 3:5b*.

"God is faithful, who will not allow you to be tempted beyond what you are able, but with the temptation will also make the way of escape, that you may be able to bear it," *1 Corinthians 10:13b*.

SOMETIMES I TRY TO SPLIT THEM UP

Jayda couldn't stand her father's new wife. It used to be that whenever Jayda and her sister, Danielle, went to stay with Dad, they could have whatever they wanted. They could rent whichever movie they liked. They could have takeout for dinner any time. They could tell Dad that they needed new clothes or shoes, and he'd take them shopping. Anything they wanted was OK with Dad.

Now that Dad had married Holly, Jayda's visits with him were not the same. Not even close. Suddenly, Dad was saying things like: "Girls, let's see what *Holly* wants to do today."

"*Holly* says that's not such a good movie for you guys to see."

STRAIGHTTALK

"*Holly* and I want to go to the other mall."

Dad had also started talking about the 'family Budget'. He wanted to start 'curbing the spending' to pay off debts.

Jayda wasn't 100% sure what he was talking about; but she had a feeling it wasn't good news as far as her wardrobe was concerned. And it seemed as if the days of takeout were over: "Holly is such a great cook. We want to start eating healthier foods."

Yeah, well, just the mention of "Holly" is enough to make me puke, Jayda thought. *So much for healthy.*

The worst part was that Dad and Holly were 'making changes to the house rules', as they put it. Chores had to be done on time. Homework had to be finished before talking on the phone. Weekend plans had to be 'approved of' first!

Next there will be guards at our front door, steamed Jayda.

Jayda was determined to drive a wedge between her stepmom and her father. *Look out, Holly. You may have messed with our territory – but Danielle and I will get it back.*

There was just one problem. Danielle actually seemed to *like* their new stepmom. She spent loads of time talking to Holly, and she was always asking Holly for help with homework. Danielle even made little presents for her.

SOMETIMES I TRY TO SPLIT THEM UP

Great! My sister is the president of the 'I love Holly' fan club, thought Jayda.

But Jayda knew that she could influence her little sister. Ever since Danielle was a baby, she'd wanted to be just like Jayda. So it was just a matter of time before Jayda swayed Danielle to her side. Now all she needed was a way to win Dad back again.

The war began. The first battlefield was the dinner table. Jayda took a bite of her dinner and made a disgusted face. Then she said rudely, "We never eat onions," as she kicked her sister under the table.

Taking the hint, Danielle dropped her fork – even though she had been wolfing down Holly's mystery meal.

Dad was not pleased. "Holly worked very hard on this meal, girls. I want you to try it." Danielle stared down at her plate, wondering what to do next.

Jayda quickly changed the direction of the conversation, so that she could play the 'Guilt Card'. She did her best to look really hurt. "Dad, I really miss those times we'd eat at that Mexican Restaurant."

Dad seemed worried. "I guess I didn't realize how much it meant to you, Sweetie."

That's all it took. The next night, the whole family piled into the car for Mexican takeout. Holly did not look very happy about it. Jayda gloated. *Success!*

STRAIGHTALK

A few days later, Jayda took a ride to the mall with her stepmom. Holly was trying to chitchat with her, as if they were girlfriends. Normally this would annoy Jayda. But today, it gave her an idea.

While they were talking, Jayda convinced Holly to get rid of some ugly old dishes that had belonged to Dad. "They're so tacky," she complained. Holly agreed, laughing.

Jayda told her stepmom that there were some cool new dishes at the mall. So they bought them, and then they took the old dishes to the thrift store. "I'm so glad you helped me pick these out!" said her new best friend Holly.

The next day, Jayda talked to Dad alone. She started to remind him of some family memories from the pre-Holly days. Soon Jayda and Dad were laughing and hugging. Right about then, she dropped the 'Holly-Bomb'.

"Dad!!! I can't believe Holly just *tossed* our dishes! As if they were nothing!"

Dad got a strange look on his face — like a trapped animal.

"Jayda, Holly just wanted to do something nice for us. I'm sure she wasn't *trying* to hurt you."

"*Nice?!* What's nice about throwing away someone's memories? Those dishes meant *so much* to Danielle and me! They reminded us of all the good times we had with you, Dad — when it was just the three of us."

SOMETIMES I TRY TO SPLIT THEM UP

Dad looked really upset. Jayda felt guilty for twisting the truth. The old dishes were hideous; they meant nothing to her. Still, she wanted to win Dad back to her side. It gave her such a feeling of *power* to know that Dad would put her needs ahead of Holly's. So she pushed the guilty feelings aside. She wanted things the way they used to be — less rules and more fun.

As the weeks passed, Jayda continued to plot against Holly. The plan seemed to be working at first. Dad was spending a lot less time trying to please Holly, and a lot more time making sure that Jayda's or Danielle's feelings weren't hurt.

Eventually, Dad and Holly began to argue. At first it was just once in awhile. Then it began happening almost every night. Dad and Holly were always cranky and restless.

One night, Jayda listened by their bedroom door as they argued. She could hear her stepmom talking to Dad: "Brad, we are husband and wife. When we make decisions together, we should stick to them. We should talk about things *together* before changing the plan."

Dad sounded frustrated. "Holly, you just don't understand. My kids have been through so much, and I just want them to have a happy life now."

Holly began to cry. "Sure, they've been through a lot. But does that make it OK to break promises to me?"

Dad sighed. "I don't know what to do; I'm always stuck in the middle. Maybe we shouldn't have gotten married — maybe it was too soon for the kids."

Jayda felt a chill run down her spine. *Did Dad actually say that?!* She wanted Dad on her side — but she'd never meant things to go this far. Jayda did not want her Dad's new marriage to end in divorce. But up until this moment, Jayda had begun to like having things go her way. *What should I do?* she wondered. The whole situation felt hopeless.

THINKING IT THROUGH

When it comes to dividing your time between parents, you may feel like a human frisbee. First Mom's house ... now Dad's ... now Mom's ... oh, wait it's time for Dad's again ... Tossing you back and forth between homes makes many parents feel incredibly guilty.

Your parents know that you would not choose to live like this. They miss you a lot during the times that you are gone. So when it is a certain parent's turn to have you at their house again – admit it — you get spoiled.

The amount of spoiling is different from household to household; it can be anywhere from moderate to mega.

Moderate spoiling is normal; most parents do this from time to time, whether or not there is a divorce involved.

But kids are smart. They know when they are getting away with things that they shouldn't — things they never would if their parents were still together.

It's easy to get used to this. Anyone can fall into the trap of trying to get away with as much as possible. Who doesn't like having their own way?

You may experience a nagging feeling about taking advantage of your parent. But you're only young once so you 'work the system' for as long as you can. Then one day, along comes a new spouse and suddenly, the party is over. Your parent begins to realize that you have been getting away with murder. The rules change – quicker than you can say 'stepfamily'!

You have two choices: accept the changes, or fight them. Logically, you know that God does not want you to disobey your parents — whether you agree with them or not, they are still in charge. And yet, should you just accept the changes as if you are fine with everything?

This is a time when you may be tempted to get your way in a less obvious style known as the 'Divide and Conquer' strategy. By driving a wedge between your parent and stepparent, you are dividing their unity. You may think that causing your parent and stepparent to argue will work to your advantage: if your parent takes your side, your problems are conquered – right?

At times it may work out that way. But you must understand that you are playing a dangerous game. God loves you too much to allow you to win at this type of game. The Bible is very clear that *no one should ever cause arguments* — also known as *strife* - between two people. This applies to any type of relationship.

In the New Testament, Jesus backs up God's law as he talks about the marriage relationship. He tells us that no one should separate what God has joined together. This means that no person should ever attempt to come between your parent and your stepparent. They are meant to be best friends to each other for life.

For certain reasons, this has already happened *once* to your parent — someone or something came between your birth parents to result in a break-up. But in this new marriage, God has blessed your parent with another chance to honor His lifelong plan for marriage. God wants this marriage to be a permanent one.

To put this in perspective, think of your own best friend. You can tell that person anything, and trust them with your secrets. They help you get through heartaches. You count on them to be there, no matter what.

But have you ever had a best friend who really let you down? Another person may have come between the two of you, so that your friend did not have as much

SOMETIMES I TRY TO SPLIT THEM UP

time for you any more. Or maybe your friend heard some talk about you that wasn't true — but believed it anyway. Your relationship was never quite the same. You felt hurt, maybe even betrayed.

Keep these painful feelings in mind for a minute. Now, multiply them by 1,000 – and you will have some idea of how hurtful these feelings are between a husband and a wife. The marriage relationship is meant to be the deepest and strongest relationship that two people can have. So when someone or something comes between them, the pain is very deep.

There will be times throughout your life when you are not happy with God's decisions. This may be one of those times. It's hard to accept changes – especially when you never asked for them.

Sometimes people make their own plans to get out of rough spots in life, rather than waiting for God to help. It may seem as if waiting for God would take too long. At times you may become so anxious to relieve your pain or discomfort that you willfully disobey God's laws. But the truth is, whenever you act outside of God's will, the hard times take even longer to improve – for everyone. God will often keep you struggling until He has your full attention again. This is because He is your loving Father. He wants you to keep your eyes on Him.

It may be hard for you to fully grasp the depth of a marriage relationship. God understands this; He does not expect you to comprehend something which you have not yet experienced. But someday, you may be married. Now is the time to begin learning how to respect and care for that special relationship.

By honoring your parent's and stepparent's decisions – rather than trying to come between them – you are showing God that you respect the marriage promises that they made to Him. This lets God know that you trust His plans. God will be pleased, and will show His approval by blessing you – no matter what changes happen at home.

TALKING WITH GOD

Dear Lord, I'm used to having things the way I like them. I know that I've gotten away with some things that I shouldn't have. Sometimes I am tempted to drive a wedge between my parent and stepparent, so that things can go back to the way they used to be. But I know that's not what You want me to do. Please show me how to respect my parent's new marriage, even on the days when I am not feeling happy about it. Amen.

MAKING CONNECTIONS

Strife can happen outside of the home, too. Sometimes, people try to split up friendships. They don't want their best friend to have any other friends; they are jealous and insecure. They may speak badly about another person, or 'forget' to include them in plans. This is selfish. If you have a friend who seems to be jealous of your other friends, talk with that person. Explain that you care about all your friends, and that they are special in different ways. Tell that person something positive about your friendship. But be firm. If the behavior does not change, make it clear that you're not OK with other friends being treated badly. A true friend does not try to hurt the people you care about.

DIGGING DEEPER

"They are no longer two but one flesh. Therefore what God has joined together, let not man separate," *Matthew 19:6*.

"Whoever digs a pit will fall into it, and he who rolls a stone will have it roll back on him," *Proverbs 26:27*.

"For My thoughts are not your thoughts, nor are your ways My ways, says the LORD. For as the heavens are higher than the earth, so are My ways higher than your ways, and My thoughts than your thoughts," *Isaiah 55:8-9*.

BURGER OR BUBBLE?

"I need two burgers up here, now! Look alive, would you?!" barked Scott's boss, Mr. Harris. "Flip those burgers, boys. If you slow down, you may as well just go home," he bellowed. Mr. Harris was a fast food tyrant. His employees secretly called him 'Burger Bully.'

Scott could not stand his job at Burger Palace. But he needed the money – and the job market for high school kids was not huge. There were a few cute girls at Burger Palace, so it wasn't completely bad. Plus he'd met Josh and Dylan there. Life was a party for those two guys. Any time Burger Bully shouted a ridiculous command, Dylan or Josh would be standing right behind him, mimicking his actions. Lately, Scott had been joining in. It made the time go by quicker; besides, it made the cute girls laugh.

Josh and Dylan were always using God's name when they swore or cussed. Apparently, cussing was funny to the cute girls. This bothered Scott. Dad had taught him to be respectful to women. Scott couldn't imagine swearing in front of any of the girls at his church. Even if he did, they definitely would not laugh and flirt with him over it. *What is up with these fast food people?*

Maybe it only bothered him because he didn't hang with many kids outside of church. *I need to catch up with the real world*, he reasoned. Scott decided that a bit of cussing wouldn't hurt. Dad will never find out. As Scott exchanged jokes and insults with Dylan and Josh, he pushed his guilt aside. Soon the cute girls began to flirt with Scott too. *Sweet!* he thought.

The restaurant slowed down. Mr. Harris walked back to his office, issuing a threat on the way. "Clean this place up if you want to keep your jobs!" he grumbled. Dylan saluted at the back of Burger Bully's head as he stormed away.

"Let's have lunch," said Josh. He snatched a cardboard French fry container and loaded it. Then he tossed a burger to one of the cute girls. She grabbed it like it was a diamond ring. Scott was worried. Cussing was one thing — but taking food, too? "Hey, guys," he began, "maybe we shouldn't be stealing this food."

Dylan laughed. "It's not stealing, you moron. It's just eating." This brilliant comment was followed by a fit of laughter from the girls.

Scott tried again. "Yeah, but we didn't pay for it. So it doesn't belong to us."

Josh scowled at him. "What's up with you? Are you one of those church people? They never have any fun."

Now the girls were making faces at him. Scott knew it was wrong to steal, but he did not want anyone making fun of him so he reached for the fries. In the back of his mind, he realized that this was the second commandment he had broken in twenty minutes. Not such a great track record.

But what was Scott supposed to do? He still had to work at Burger Palace almost every day. None of the other kids were 'church people.' *So maybe I'll just do whatever it takes to fit in while I'm at work*, he reasoned. *Then I'll follow God's rules the rest of the time. Maybe that's what people have to do in life — live in two separate worlds.* But as Scott tried to convince himself that this is what life was about, he felt a nagging feeling that God would disagree.

THINKING IT THROUGH

Nobody can live in a bubble. People may pretend that they don't need any world outside of the church door, but that's impossible. Everywhere you turn, the world is there. And much of it is a world without God. There is no God allowed in public schools, or most workplaces. There is no hint of God's law in most television programs, books, movies or video games. Advertisements are focused on everything but the word of God.

It is hard enough being a teen. Who wants to stick out like a neon sign that screams 'Ten Commandments Only'? Everyone wants to have friends. You've probably felt like Scott did at one time or another – in order to survive, maybe you need to become two separate people: the 'Christian You', and the 'Real World You.'

A long time ago, a guy named Elimelech did the same thing. Elimelech believed in God, and he lived in the land of Judah. He had a wife and two sons. But there was a famine in Judah. Soon there was not enough food or water for everyone. Elimelech didn't want his family to starve, so he took them to the country of Moab.

Moab was a pagan country. The lifestyle in Moab was completely opposite to God's laws. Elimelech planned to keep his family in Moab until the famine passed and then take them home, but they ended up staying for ten years.

BURGER OR BUBBLE?

You belong on solid ground. Elimelech belonged on solid ground too. When he lived in Judah, he had people close by who would pray for him and help him get back on track. Elimelech was never meant to stay in Moab. There was no one there who cared about the one true God. So there was no more bubble to protect Elimelech's sons. They grew up in the 'real' world – and eventually, they joined it. Elimelech's sons married Moabite girls – which was definitely against God's word. Then Elimelech and his sons died, leaving his wife Naomi behind.

Not everyone in the real world is bad. Take Ruth, for instance. Ruth had been married to one of Elimelech's sons. She was a Moabite. But she would not leave Naomi. Instead, she moved to Judah with her. She chose to leave behind her 'real' world and follow God's word.

So if believers can sometimes make bad choices – and non-believers are often good to others – then which kind of people make better friends? It may seem crazy to choose one world or the other. After all, they overlap so much.

But think of it this way: there is a big difference between a human and a frog. That's right, a frog. But what do frogs have to do with faith? More than you think. A frog is amphibious – designed to live on land and in the water. You are not. You may swim in the water from time to time, but you must live on solid ground.

As a Christian you also have two 'worlds'. There is the world that is against God and the world that is for God. The world that is for God is sometimes called God's Kingdom or Heaven. It is the world that you belong to when you trust in the Lord Jesus Christ. However, as you live day by day in the other world you are still part of that world, it's just that you should not be ruled by it – you should be ruled by God and His word.

So you are in one world day by day – the so-called 'real' world: at school, work and in your neighborhood. In that world you will feel tempted, or even pressured, to give in to all of the things that this real world has to offer. But this real world is not your real home. When you begin to hang out with non-Christian friends, it can become very easy to forget the teachings of God. You will meet some very friendly non-Christian people, but here's the thing – since they do not know God, they will not stop to think whether He would approve of their actions. Before you know it, you could stop seeking God's approval as well.

Be smart when you choose friends. Be friendly to Christians and non-Christians. However, pray each day that God will bring friends into your life who will help you keep His word in your heart. Ask Him for the strength to do the right thing – even when you are outside of the bubble. This way, when you do go for a swim with non-believers, you will always keep your solid ground in sight.

TALKING WITH GOD
Father God, sometimes it seems too hard to be a Christian around other kids who do not believe. I want to fit in. But I also want to follow You. Please give me the strength to make the right choices. I want to have friends who will not lead me away from you. Amen.

MAKING CONNECTIONS
What are things like where you work or go to school? Maybe you are one of those people who is really good at remembering God's word — wherever you are. That is an awesome gift. Be thankful for it. But there will still be times when you try to convince yourself that something you are doing isn't that bad - compared to what other kids do. Don't fall into that trap. No matter how small the sin may seem, it still matters to God.

Pick one Scripture verse that really means something to you - something that reminds you that God is your solid ground. Then write it on a small piece of paper and keep it somewhere that you can read it a lot - like your wallet, your locker door, or your mirror. When you keep God's word close by, you will always remember where you belong.

DIGGING DEEPER

"...And they went to the country of Moab and remained there," *Ruth 1:2*.

"Deliver me speedily; be my rock of refuge," *Psalm 31:2*.

"Whoever comes to Me, and hears My sayings and does them, I will show you whom he is like: He is like a man building a house, who dug deep and laid the foundation on the rock. And when the flood arose, the stream beat vehemently against that house, and could not shake it, for it was founded on the rock," *Luke 6:47-48*.

MOM LETS ME DO IT

Ty remembered at the last minute to hide the CD he'd just bought. *I don't need any lectures today*, he thought as he jammed it into his backpack. His stepmom Sharon was always inspecting the music he listened to.

Last week he bought a new rap CD, and made the mistake of leaving it on the kitchen counter. Sharon threw it away while he was at school. What was that about?! It was his money, not hers. Why couldn't he spend it the way he wanted to?

Sometimes Dad checked out Ty's music too; but he was a lot cooler about it. If Dad didn't approve of the music, he would just take Ty back to the store to get the 'edited version' of the CD.

Ty understood Dad's point. He knew that the words of his favorite songs were not exactly church-friendly. *But I'm not stupid*, he thought. *I know how I'm supposed to live. It's just that I like how the music sounds.*

Sharon's privacy invasion did not stop at Ty's CD rack. She also thought it was OK to look through the rest of Ty's room whenever she wanted to. If Sharon found anything that she didn't approve of — movies, games, whatever — she'd chew him out once he got home from school. Unbelievable.

Ty complained to Dad about his stepmom's snooping habit. But Dad didn't seem too concerned about it. He actually said that 'all parents do that from time to time'.

Dad must have been brainwashed by Sharon.

When Ty stayed with his mom, things were a lot easier. She let Ty decide which music he listened to, which movies he watched and which video games he played. Mom never asked where Ty was going, or when he was coming home.

She didn't even hassle him if Ty skipped church on Sundays. Why should she? She never went either. Once in awhile, Mom even let Ty have a beer. *Sharon would have a heart attack if she knew that!* Ty laughed to himself.

Sometimes Mom would try to help Ty when he got into trouble with Dad and Sharon. She'd call Dad and ask him to ease up. Dad did not back down very often. Still, Ty liked knowing that Mom was on his side.

Ty could not figure out Dad's sudden interest in creating the perfect church family. When Ty was a little kid, his parents were really involved at church. But in the last few years before the divorce, Mom stopped going to church. Dad didn't seem to care so much about the Bible either. At least he didn't act like it.

Then Dad met Sharon, and he suddenly cranked up the volume on the whole church thing. He started taking Ty there every week, and he joined the men's bible study. Then Dad went on a retreat! To Ty, it seemed as if an alien had come and traded places with his father.

After the wedding, Dad went full-blast. Now he insisted that Ty join them for 'family' devotionals once a week. Ty barely knew Sharon; why would he want to do devotionals with her?! *Big difference between Mom's house and this one*, Ty thought as he turned the doorknob.

Once he was in the house, he knew that something was up. Sharon was on the phone, and she looked furious. As soon as she saw Ty, she told the person on the other end: "I have to go. He's here now."

Nice to see you too, Ty thought sarcastically.

"That was your father on the phone," Sharon announced.

Ty said nothing. How was he supposed to answer that?

Sharon looked as if she would start spewing hot lava out the top of her head. The visual made Ty laugh. Not such a good move at the moment.

Sharon glared at him. "You won't be smirking in a few minutes, Mister! Your father is on the way home now."

Ty's smile disappeared as an alarm went off in his brain.

That can't be good. Dad never comes home early from work.

Ty didn't feel like being stared down until Dad got home. So he grabbed the cordless phone to call Mom while he was waiting. Mom had a way of seeing the humor in Ty's battles with his stepmom.

Sharon blocked his path. "And who do you think *you're* calling?" she demanded.

"My mom," Ty said, looking her straight in the eye. "Is that a *problem*?"

"Whatever, Ty. Call your mother. But I don't think she'll be bailing you out this time."

What does she have on me? Ty wondered. Besides the CD in his backpack, he couldn't think of anything else he had done that was against the rules. But with Sharon, it seemed like there was always *something* he wasn't doing right.

"You know, maybe there's a reason my mom bails me out. Maybe all your rules are just crazy," Ty replied.

Unfortunately, at that moment Dad walked in.

"Ty Robertson! You might get away with talking back to your mom, but do not speak that way in this house!"

Ty was tired of it. "You know what, Dad? I don't ever *need* to talk to Mom that way, because she doesn't treat me like a kid who's headed for Juvenile Hall, the way you and Sharon do!"

"Sharon and I have rules because we care about you — who you are now, and who you will become. Your mother, on the other hand, lets you get away with whatever you want!" Dad exploded.

"My mother *trusts* me to make my own choices, Dad. Which is more than I can say for you!" shouted Ty.

"Your father will trust you when you can show him that you are worthy of his trust," added Sharon.

"Funny how he never had a problem trusting me before *you* showed up. You have no reason to accuse me the way you do," Ty answered.

"Then how do you explain *this* being in your hockey bag?" Sharon asked, holding up an unopened can of beer.

Ty stared at the can that he had totally forgotten about.

125

What could he say? He was nailed.

A few weeks ago Mom's boyfriend, Alex, brought him a beer while he was studying for a huge trigonometry test. Ty didn't even want the beer. He didn't think it was right to drink it, especially on a school night. It would make him tired, and then he wouldn't study.

At the time, Ty took the beer and said thanks, not wanting to look like a lightweight; but when Alex left the room, Ty put it in his hockey bag. He meant to put it back in the fridge later, but he got so wrapped up in his trig notes that he completely forgot about it.

Ty tried to figure a way to get out of trouble. He could explain it to Dad and Sharon; but he doubted they would believe him. He could ask Mom or Alex to back him up; but that was dumb because he would feel like a loser if Alex found out that he hid the beer.

Instead, Ty took the defensive approach. "Do I go through *your* stuff? *Do I*? No! Then why should you go through mine?"

"Where did you get it, Ty?" insisted Dad.

Finally Ty let loose. "At Mom's house, OK? Mom and Alex let me have a beer once in awhile, because they *trust me*. Just like Mom trusts me to choose my own music, and games, and movies. I'm almost an adult, Dad! What's the major big deal?!"

Sharon stepped in. "The major big deal is that we are Christians, and your mother has chosen not to be. Your dad and I are trying to raise you to follow Christ, not the rest of the world."

Dad's face looked calmer as he put his hand on Ty's shoulder. "Becoming an adult does not mean just doing whatever you want, Ty; it means that you are learning to make responsible choices."

He knew that Dad's words made sense. But it seemed to Ty that being a Christian was much more of a hassle than living like the rest of the world lived. He hated the constant pressure he was under at his father's house. Living at Mom's was much easier.

Yet Ty knew that the way he lived while he was at Mom's house did not always please God. That bothered him. Ty wasn't sure which way he wanted to live. Either way, he was glad that he never drank that beer.

THINKING IT THROUGH

How is it possible that two adults could have two completely different views of what is right and wrong? It's enough to make you crazy. But it is all too common, especially when one parent is not following the Lord.

For the non-Christian parent — as in the case of Ty's mom — morals are decided based on personal interpretation of what's right and what's wrong. Rules are made according to what the world says is OK.

For the parent who is walking with the Lord, like Ty's dad, there is only one set of rules – the ones in the Bible. These rules apply to everyone, and they do not change from situation to situation. Hmmm...which set of rules sounds easier to follow?

God's rules are especially hard to follow if you try to live with one foot in each world. Here is an example: If you tell a lie, the worldly view might be that it's OK, as long as you do it to spare someone's feelings. If you ask friends for advice, they would probably tell you that the lie is OK in your case. Since you want your friends' approval – and don't want to risk hurting someone's feelings – you lean towards telling the lie.

But then you open your Bible. God says that telling a lie is not OK. Ever. Period. So in spite of how much easier it would be to tell the lie, God commands you to take the hard road. You are supposed to tell the truth, in spite of what the rest of the world would think.

In the end, God's laws are there for your good, and the good of others. He did not make up rules to make life hard. He did it to protect you from harm. Remember this as you compare the rules in each of your homes.

Like Ty, you may feel that life is easier with fewer rules.

MOM LETS ME DO IT

But is it right to get away with things, just because you can? Ask yourself: Who is it really helping when I get away with things? Is it hurting me or someone else? What does God say about following the rules?

Jesus understands what it is like to be tempted. Once, when He was on a mountain fasting and praying, Satan tempted Him in all kinds of ways. Satan knew that Jesus was alone, tired and weak – and out of other people's sight. It is easier to give into temptation when you think you won't be caught! Even when no one is around to see our sins, God still knows what we have done.

In the home with more rules, it may seem like your new stepparent is coming down hard on you. But consider this: is it possible that your attitude toward your stepparent may be part of the problem? Have you weighed out the rules, and the reasons they have for setting them? If you have been treated unfairly, have you tried to point this out in a respectful way?

Think carefully. There are probably valid points on both sides – yours and your parents'. Maybe each side needs to bend a little. Talking is a good way to start.

It is not easy to choose the hard road. But the more often you read the Bible and pray, the easier it will be to make right choices. God strengthens His children when they set out to do the right thing. Instead of asking yourself why there are two sets of rules, ask yourself: *which set of rules is best to follow?*

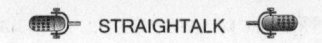

TALKING WITH GOD

Dear God, thank you that I have the Bible as my rule book. Help me to do what is right, even when it is easy to get away with doing the wrong thing. Lord, I need some help with my parents. I feel that I am not trusted, and I am not sure how to handle this. Please help me find a way to show my parents that I can be trusted. Amen.

MAKING CONNECTIONS

Divorced parents are not the only ones who may send mixed messages about right and wrong. Even with married birth parents, one may be strict when you break the rules, while the other one rarely punishes you. It's not your fault that they handle things differently; but you do have a choice in the way that you respond. God knows that you are old enough to understand the difference between right and wrong. So if you break a rule, don't run to the 'easy' parent, whining to get out of a punishment. This dishonors the other parent. Besides, although you may not like having a punishment, you've earned it – no one made you break the rule. Rather than breaking a rule next time, ask your parents if you can talk about it. Give them your ideas for an alternative. Even if they do not change their minds, you have still shown your parents that you are trying to be honest and responsible. The more they see those qualities in you, the more likely they are to trust you.

DIGGING DEEPER

"The eyes of the LORD are in every place, keeping watch on the evil and the good," *Proverbs 15:3.*

"Enter by the narrow gate; for wide is the gate and broad is the way that leads to destruction, and there are many who go in by it," *Matthew 7:13.*

"And do not be conformed to this world, but be transformed by the renewing of your mind, that you may prove what is that good and acceptable and perfect will of God," *Romans 12:2.*

CUT AND RUN

Mae could not believe that she would have to speak in front of the whole history class — again. The first time was in the fall, when the class learned about China. Mrs. Garrett told the students to report on their favorite topic in Chinese history. That should have been incredibly easy for her — being that her grandfather was born there. Except for one thing — the students had to share their information in front of the entire room.

Mae worried so much that she got absolutely no sleep the night before her presentation. She knew that she had dark circles under her eyes. And her hands were shaking so bad when she put on her lipstick that she smeared it onto her chin. Even though she wiped it off, a pink dot was still showing. This made her look like a sloppy little kid who had just eaten strawberry ice cream.

But the worst part was when she opened her mouth to speak. Nothing came out. Everyone was staring at her, wondering why she was taking so long to say something. Then they started laughing at her. Mae wanted to crawl under her desk. But Mrs. Garrett insisted that she take a deep breath and begin. This time, Mae spoke — but her voice came out very high-pitched and shaky, like the witch's voice in the Wizard of Oz.

This time around, she had to research the French Revolution. Why was public speaking so important to Mrs. Garrett? Mae could write a paper about almost anything — so why did she have to speak in front of the class to prove that she knew history? Why did she ever have to speak in front of a crowd about anything, ever?

Mae's friend Casey saw the horrified look on her face. "What are you going to do?" Casey asked.

"I don't know — quit school?" Mae joked, although nothing about this project was funny. She noticed many of the other students whispering and pointing to her. Apparently, they expected another episode of the 'Wizard of Oz.' *Super*, thought Mae.

At the end of the day, Mae went to see Mrs. Garrett. She was hoping to change her teacher's mind. "Mrs.

Garrett, I really don't want to do this project in front of the room. Couldn't I just do a paper, or an extra assignment? Anything – please," begged Mae.

But Mrs. Garrett would not budge. In fact, Mae's request seemed to irritate her. "Mae, some time you will just need to grow up. You are not a small child. You should be able to give a speech by now without melting into a puddle of water."

Mae walked away in defeat. What could she possibly say to that? Mae's teacher was just as mean as her classmates. It was as if all of her hard work and good grades never mattered at all.

Mae couldn't tell her family. She hadn't told them about the disastrous China speech either. She remembered how proud her grandfather had been when he'd read her research. He would probably be so ashamed if he knew how awful her speech was. That's why she had to keep this project to herself too.

Mae tried to focus on her research all week – but every time she started to choose a topic, she thought about how much she dreaded speaking in front of the class. Her mother noticed that she was not eating much at dinner. "Are you feeling sick, Mae?" she asked. Her grandfather looked at Mae as if he knew she was hiding something. But Mae kept it to herself. Even when Casey called her to ask how her project was turning out, Mae just changed the subject.

Soon the dreaded day had arrived — and Mae had not finished her project. She was not even halfway through. Mae panicked when her mother called her to come downstairs. "Coming!" she yelled nervously.

Mae knew what she had to do. She would cut history class. In fact, she would cut the whole day of school. She would use Casey's cell phone to call the school. She could pretend to be her mother and say, "My daughter, Mae, is very sick." Maybe she would even do that for two days in a row. By then, all of the speeches for Mrs. Garrett's class would be finished. Then Mae would return to school and hand in her written history project. *I feel better already*, she thought. *I just hope I can pull this off.*

Casey didn't mind if Mae borrowed her phone — but she was really nervous when she realized what her friend was up to. Once Mae hung up, Casey shrieked, "Mae! Did you just pretend to be your mom? You're really not going to school? You'll get in so much trouble!"

"Not if I don't get caught," Mae said. "Casey, please don't tell. You know I can't speak in front of the whole room. It will work out — you'll see."

Casey looked worried — but she hugged Mae and

CUT AND RUN

then walked to school. Mae put on some sunglasses and walked in the opposite direction. *But where do I go?* she wondered. Finally, she saw a coffee shop. She went in and piled her books into a corner chair. Then she turned her back toward the window. Mae settled in to work on her project, keeping her dark glasses on.

An hour and one hot tea later, Mae heard a familiar voice at the counter. "One latte with soy milk, please." It was Mr. Davis, the principal of Mae's school!

Oh, no! Mae thought as she hunched over her books. *Maybe he won't notice me?*

The girl behind the counter recognized the principal. "Good morning! I thought you would be sleeping in today, being that school is closed," she chirped.

Mr. Davis looked puzzled. "School is not closed today. What gave you that idea?"

The girl looked confused. "Well, I thought I saw a high school kid studying back there."

Mr. Davis said, "Excuse me for a moment," as he headed in Mae's direction. There was nowhere she could run. The best Mae could hope for was that he wouldn't recognize her behind her shades. But he did.

"Mae Wu?" he asked. "Aren't you the girl who won the essay contest this fall?"

"Yes," Mae answered as she felt a million butterflies

in her stomach. *That's one contest I regret winning*, she thought.

"Then why aren't you in school today?" he asked angrily. When Mae didn't answer, he pulled up a chair. "Mae, you are a very good student. This isn't like you. Talk to me." His face now looked more concerned than angry.

Suddenly, Mae found herself explaining the whole thing – the China project, her grandfather, the 'Wizard of Oz' voice and the other students laughing. Then she moved on to the latest history project. Mae felt a bit like a criminal in a court case, proving that she had no choice but to break the law.

When she was finished speaking, the principal was silent for a long time. Finally he said, "Mae, I understand why you were upset. Thanks for explaining everything to me. But cutting school is against the law. We will have to call your family."

Mae was horrified. Now her grandfather would definitely be ashamed of her. Her mother would be so angry. Mae wondered if her classmates would find out that she'd cut school. Great – there's one more thing they'll have to laugh about, she realized. She hadn't solved her problem after all – she'd made it bigger.

THINKING IT THROUGH

Fear can really limit people. Many fears are based upon what people don't do well. Since everyone is wired with different talents, likes and dislikes, there are bound to be some things you can't do well. Some things are not an issue very often. Suppose you are not so great at hockey; then you only need to be concerned with your skill level if you are on a rink. But other things are a bigger part of daily life – in school, at home or at work. Sometimes you will fail at those things – and failure can be very embarrassing. No one likes to be laughed at.

Moses was a great leader of the Israelites. But did you know that Moses was afraid to speak in public? He had a speech disability. But God wanted Moses to speak to Pharaoh and his entire court; and at other times, to all of the Israelites. Like Mae, Moses looked for a way out. He should have known that God would give him the strength to work through his weaknesses – and God did do this.

When you are afraid of something, it's tempting to run from the problem. Mae figured that if she didn't risk trying, then she wouldn't fail. And if she didn't fail, she wouldn't get hurt. That didn't get her very far. Whenever you try to bury a problem, it eventually pokes its head out of the ground, and the situation gets more and more complicated. In Mae's case, not only did she cut class, lie and hide;

she also asked Casey to help her sin.

There was a time when King David had committed a huge sin – and then asked a friend to help him cover it up. David fell in love with Bathsheba, the wife of his most loyal soldier. Bathsheba ended up pregnant, and David was afraid to face up to what he had done. So he asked his friend Joab to send the soldier out to the front lines, and then leave him unprotected so he would be killed. Even though it was not Joab's fault that Bathsheba was pregnant, or that David had asked him to help with the cover-up, Joab was still guilty. He had helped David to sin.

There will be times in life when you can't avoid a scary moment. If you are afraid, don't trick yourself into thinking that running away or covering up will solve your problem. Instead, ask God for strength. He gives us the strength we need through prayer, through His word and through good friends who encourage us.

Even though God is our Deliverer, He does not take away everything we dislike. A scary problem can be like a fire. God always hears our prayers to be delivered from the fire – but He does not always answer our prayers in the way that we expect. Sometimes God keeps the fire from happening at all. Other times the fire happens, but then He puts it out right away. But there will always be times when God wants us to walk through the fire. He will put His arms around us and protect us — but we will still be walking through it.

God does not make you walk through fires because He wants to scare you. He does it so you can grow stronger in your faith and in your skills. The struggles that you are going through right now are part of God's plan for your future. Perhaps you will meet someone who needs your help. You will be able to help this person in their struggles because you have struggled yourself. You are a useful part of His big plan in this world. So don't run from troubles — run to God.

TALKING WITH GOD

Dear Lord, there's something going on in my life right now that I fear. I am so tempted to run from the issue or cover it up — because I don't want to be embarrassed, or get into trouble. That's so hard, God. Please deliver me. But help me to trust that whichever way You deliver me is the best way. Amen.

MAKING CONNECTIONS

Maybe you've been in Casey's shoes. You want to be a good friend, so you have lied to keep a friend out of trouble. When you care about people, you don't like to see them get hurt. But getting hurt is a part of life. If you really want to be the best friend you can be, help your friends to become stronger. Be there to listen while they go through hard or embarrassing times. Offer suggestions for working through the issues. A card or a note can show someone that you are there to help. Sometimes just hanging out with them is more important than any advice. And of course, you can pray for them.

Sometimes friends may come to you after they have done something harmful; but they want you to keep it a secret. This is not a good idea. Tell them how much you care about them, and encourage them to admit what they've done. Then pray for them to do the right thing. If they do not confess, then ask a trusted adult for advice. Your friend may become angry with you for sharing their secret. But it is better to have them angry with you than to risk more harm later on.

DIGGING DEEPER

"Then Moses said to the LORD, 'O my Lord ... I am slow of speech and slow of tongue.' So the LORD said to him, 'Who has made man's mouth? Or who makes the mute, the deaf, the seeing, or the blind? Have not I, the LORD? Now therefore, go, and I will be with your mouth and teach you what you shall say,'" *Exodus 4:10-12*.

"In the morning it happened that David wrote a letter to Joab...and he wrote in the letter, saying, 'Set Uriah in the forefront of the hottest battle, and retreat from him, that he may be struck down and die,'" *2 Samuel 11:14-15*.

"I sought the LORD, and He heard me, and delivered me from all my fears," *Psalm 34:4*.

STUCK IN THE MIDDLE

"So, how's Dork-Pants today?" teased Jason's father over the phone. Dad was always quick to point out other people's flaws - especially when it came to Jason's new stepfather, Ron.

"He's OK, I guess," answered Jason, hoping Dad would move on to a new topic now.

He didn't.

"Did you tell him that his clothes went out of style with Duran Duran?" joked Dad, laughing to himself.

"Uh - What's Duran Duran?" Jason asked.

"Music group from the 1980s. Never mind, Jay. They made the charts before you were born. Old news! Like Ronnie Boy."

Jason tried to change the conversation direction.

"Yeah, well, Phil Collins was around before I was born too. Not exactly my speed, but *he* still makes the charts."

Unfortunately, Dad was not ready to let up on the Ron-bashing.

"So what does that mean? You think ol' Ronnie is a chart-buster now? If I didn't know better, I'd think you were sticking up for him."

Jason held the receiver away from his ear. He was really tempted to just hang up. Instead he took a deep breath. He thought of another way to change the subject, and tried again.

"Hey Dad, my team won again last night. Now we're 5 and 0. Not bad, huh?"

"That's my boy!" Dad said proudly. "Sorry I couldn't be there. Did you score any touchdowns?"

"A *major* one. No one can believe I pulled it off. Brandon had the ball, and then..."

Dad interrupted. "Did your mother get to see it?"

"Uh ... yeah," Jason answered slowly. He had a feeling he knew what was coming next, so he kept talking to distract Dad. "So anyway, remember that big dude from the other team – Mark Layton? Well he starts tearing after Brandon..."

Dad cut him off again. "Was your StepDork there?"

STUCK IN THE MIDDLE

Who cares if Ron was there! thought Jason angrily.

"Hey Dad, do you want to hear the story, or not?"

Dad kept at it. "Why was Ron there? He doesn't even *like* football."

Jason picked up his football and threw it against the wall. "Well maybe he likes *me*, Dad! Did you ever think of that?! And how would you know whether or not he likes football?"

"Come on, Jay..."

"No, *you* come on, Dad!" answered Jason, raising his voice. "You know what? At least he was there!!!"

Jason knew that last comment was mean. It wasn't as if Dad was always missing-in-action. Jason knew that his father had gotten stuck at work last night.

It's just that he was so sick of hearing Dad trash Ron. In the beginning, Jason used to join in. But lately, he'd been feeling bad about it. Maybe Ron wasn't so smooth, but he was basically a good guy.

Now it was Dad's turn to freak. "Yeah, well, this phone call just ended. I can see you've got more important people in your life now!"

Jason heard a dial tone. He slammed down the receiver. He wondered if he'd always be stuck in the middle between his dad and his stepfather.

He did a mental pro-and-con list of the two men.

On the one hand, Jason had Dad, who was loud and opinionated; maybe 'obnoxious' would be a better word. But Dad always knew how to have fun. Jason was never bored when they were together.

On the other hand, there was Ron. Ron's idea of a good time was watching the Nature Channel. But Jason noticed that Ron never talked badly about Dad, no matter how rude Dad was to him. And Dad could get *very* rude when he wanted to. Jason had to give his stepdad credit for putting up with all that.

Dad was the one who chose to leave; so why couldn't he just suck it up and deal with the fact that there was a different guy in the house now?

It was like Dad and Ron were two rival teams. Which team was Jason supposed to play for? Lately he felt less like a football player — and more like a referee.

THINKING IT THROUGH

You've been trying your best to get along with your stepparent, for your parent's sake. It's not like you had a vote in their marriage, but the least you can do is make the effort to be friendly, right? Who knows, maybe something good can come of it. And yet, you want to be loyal to the parent who is no longer in the home. It's not like you want to replace them or anything. But you worry that they will see it that way.

And guess what? They probably will.

Even the most self-confident parents in the world feel a little insecure now and then – especially after a divorce. Your parents may feel some guilt or shame at causing a painful change in your life.

One parent remarries. Suddenly there is a new person in your life; with any luck, maybe they are fun, young or cool. Or maybe he or she is great at things that your 'real' parent – the one who doesn't live there anymore – is not.

And now this person gets to see you all the time. At times, they will get to ask you about your day before you have even had a chance to tell your 'real' parent about it. And even then, the 'real' parent will hear about it over the phone, not in person.

What a head-trip for your parent. Imagine how they must feel, knowing all of this. Can you blame them for feeling jealous?

Everyone feels jealous from time to time. Jealousy can cause people to say or do things that they may regret later. Emotions can sometimes be hard to control.

It's what people *do* about their jealousy that either prevents trouble, or causes it. There are basically two options: turn to God in prayer, or turn into an ugly monster.

Jason's dad missed him. He could no longer be with his son every day, and he began to feel really insecure that Ron might be taking over his role in Jason's life. So Jason's father tried to cover up his fear with humor. By making fun of Ron, he figured that he was making himself look better.

But it had the exact opposite effect. Jason's dad trashed Ron so often that it got annoying. Soon, Jason didn't even enjoy talking to his dad. So the jealousy problem was not solved; unfortunately, it ended up causing even more problems.

Does your parent bash your stepparent? Not good. This is called *slander*, and God is not OK with it. Slander is a really dangerous way to handle a problem; it can trick even the nicest people into becoming the meanest people. Put-downs are always wrong, whether we do it straight up or disguise it as a joke.

But hang in there; there is hope. God loves your parent, and He understands that it is very difficult for them to adjust to the new marriage. This is especially true if your parent did not want the first marriage to end.

God is very pleased with you in this matter. Why? Because you chose to listen to that feeling in the pit of your stomach — the one that tells you that slander is not cool. You are experiencing something called *conviction*.

Conviction is a gift from God. It helps us remember what is right and wrong, so that when we are tempted, we will make a godly choice.

Now that you understand that slander is not OK, it's time to help your parent tune in too. Timing is everything here. Remember, your parent is hurting – they feel less important in your life. You definitely need to address the issue; just make sure you don't tackle them with it.

The best way to do this is to plan some quality time. Your parent is likely to be in a great mood if you are doing something together. After an hour or so, bring up the issue. Be kind – it is possible that your parent really did not stop to think about how they were behaving, or that maybe it was making you uncomfortable.

If your parent says that they will try not to trash your new stepparent anymore, great! You might want to ask them if it's alright to remind them whenever they start to do it in the future. If you've been respectful up to this point, then they will probably be cool about that.

If things do not go smoothly, don't push it. An argument is not what you are after. Even if you don't agree with your parent's thoughts or actions, you still need to show respect for them. So it's best to just drop the subject for now.

If your parent does not respond as you had hoped,

remember that they may have been a little embarrassed to have their flaws pointed out. We can all relate to that! Or maybe it's just that they have been caught off-guard; they might need time to think things over. After all, the gift of conviction is for adults too! Don't worry, you aren't the referee – God is.

TALKING TO GOD

Dear Father, thank you for the gift of conviction, so that I can make the right choices. Right now my parent is feeling jealous, and it's causing some problems with my stepparent. I don't want to get stuck in the middle. Help me talk to my parent about this, and even if my parent continues to talk badly about my stepparent, please help me to avoid the temptation to join in. Amen.

MAKING CONNECTIONS

You may feel this way about friends at times too. Two people may be angry at each other, and you care about them both. Even though you are not involved in their disagreement, each one wants you to hear their story and choose their side. The next time you notice this happening, avoid getting caught in the middle. Stop your friend before the venting starts. Explain that you are friends with both of them, and you'd like it to stay that way. Encourage that friend to talk to the other person, rather than you. Offer to pray with them for a solution.

DIGGING DEEPER

"You desire truth in the inward parts, and in the hidden part You will make me to know wisdom," *Psalm 51:6*.

"A sound heart is life to the body, but envy is rottenness to the bones," *Proverbs 14:30*.

"There is one who speaks like the piercings of a sword, but the tongue of the wise promotes health," *Proverbs 12:18*.

MAKE WAY FOR BABY

"Hey, Clarissa — which color would be better? Pink or lavender?" called Mom from the spare bedroom.

Clarissa sighed. *More baby plans. Great!* she thought sarcastically.

"Pink," she answered. Clarissa's favorite color was purple. She had to have *something* that set her apart from the baby.

Mom was due in three months. The baby would be a girl. Mom and her new husband, Rich, were jazzed about it. Rich's two sons seemed cool with it too, even though they had been hoping for a baby brother. Other than that, it seemed as if the baby was no big deal to Todd and Zach.

What's wrong with me? Clarissa wondered. *Mom waited so long for the right guy. Now Rich is here, and they're happy. So why do I feel weird about this baby?*

She went to talk to Mom. Whenever Clarissa was uneasy about something, having a heart-to-heart with her mother made her feel better. Mom was good at listening. She had this great way of seeing a problem from all sides, so that Clarissa could figure out the best solution. But this time she couldn't tell Mom what her trouble was about. How could she?

Uh, Mom, I'm not OK with you having another baby. Especially a girl. So how can we solve this? Sure. That would go over big.

Clarissa stood in the doorway and picked up a little pink mouse. "This is cute, Mom," she said.

Mom smiled. "It used to be yours."

That really bothered Clarissa. *What if I still wanted it?* she thought. *Not that I have any use for it, but that's not the point...*

"How was school, Babe?" Mom asked.

Clarissa went over the day in her mind before answering. Clarissa had a major crush on Josh. *But Josh likes Cami Flynn - not me!* She wanted to talk about it with Mom, but she wasn't sure where to start. Talking about it seemed to make it hurt more.

While Clarissa was deep in thought about her day, Mom moved on to a new topic. "I got three little dresses for the baby today with matching socks! It's going to be so much fun having a baby girl to dress!"

"Um, Mom ... you already had that with *me*, remember?" Clarissa answered.

Mom rubbed her belly. "Of course I do, Babe! But that was so long ago. Now it's all new again!"

Clarissa felt a stab of pain. *Yeah, so long ago. Old news.*

"So, Mom ...," she began, wanting to tell her about Josh.

"Oh!" Mom interrupted. "I was thinking of having Rich paint the room this weekend — that's why I asked you 'pink or lavender' — and I was wondering if you'd like to help us." That made Clarissa feel strange. Before Mom married Rich, she and Clarissa had automatically done everything together. They'd basically been alone since Clarissa was a baby. 'Our tiny family of two', as Mom liked to put it.

Clarissa had actually liked it that way. Sure, she and Mom never had much money. And it was really lonely sometimes; Clarissa had always wished for a dad. But she and Mom took care of each other. Over the years, they had become really close.

Suddenly the days of Mom and Clarissa were over. Now, it was Mom and Rich. Clarissa felt like she was just tagging along.

"Sure, Mom. I'll help you," Clarissa finally replied. She decided to try bringing up the Josh issue again.

"Hey, Mom, about school..."

But Mom was on baby-autopilot. "Do you think she'll look like me, or Rich? Or maybe she'll look like *you!*" she exclaimed cheerfully.

Clarissa lost it. "How special, Mom! Then my existence will be totally unnecessary!" she responded.

"Clarissa! Why would you say that?" Mom asked, looking hurt.

"Well, I've been trying to talk to you about my day for about twenty minutes now, and all you keep talking about is the baby!" explained Clarissa.

Mom tucked Clarissa's hair behind her ear. "I'm sorry, Babe, it just seemed like you didn't want to talk about school..."

"*Mom,*" Clarissa cut in, "today is not the first time this has happened. Ever since you found out about the baby, you have been totally out of it. I can't even talk to you anymore."

Mom looked upset. "Sweetie, I wasn't trying to push you aside. Please try to understand, this is a big deal for Rich and me. She's our first baby together, and she's Rich's first little girl."

"But she's not *your* first girl, Mom. You already have one. She's been standing right in front of you, but you haven't seen her for months!" Clarissa cried.

Is this the way it was going to be from now on? Clarissa knew that she should be excited about the baby, but she just wasn't into the whole idea. Instead of gaining a sister, she felt more like she was losing her identity.

THINKING IT THROUGH

If you've experienced life in a one-parent household, you know that there are many ups and downs. You help each other through struggles in a way that outsiders just can't. Only the people in your own family can understand the things you have been through. In the long run, this brings all of you closer together than many families who have never lost a parent.

Once you have bonded in this way, it can be very hard to let someone else come into the group. They are not part of the family history. They haven't experienced the pain that you and your parent have.

It's not so much that you don't want them in the family; in fact, you may have even prayed that they would come along some day. But the closeness you share with your parent has become special to you. You have come to rely on your parent, just as your parent has relied on you. You understand each other on a very deep level, and you don't want that special bond to be broken.

Clarissa was feeling that way about Rich. She did not dislike him, yet he was bonding with her mother in a way that felt *threatening* to Clarissa. She feared that her relationship with her mother would be replaced by the marriage.

A new baby in a stepfamily can cause even more anxiety and envy than a new stepparent. For one thing, the baby will not be a stepkid of either parent. This means that this child will never really experience the same sort of troubles that you have had in the family. Plus, the baby's parents live together in the same house. This child will not have the stress of wondering if a no-show parent will finally make an appearance. And there will be no shuffling between two homes.

Most of all, the new baby's parents love each other. The pregnancy and birth will strengthen that bond even more. The baby is a living, breathing reminder of their unity.

There is a family in the Bible who went through a similar struggle. A man named Jacob was married to a woman named Leah. He had some children with Leah. But

MAKE WAY FOR BABY

later he married a woman named Rachel, whom he had always loved. After a really long wait, Rachel and Jacob were finally able to have a son. The new baby — Joseph — was really special to Jacob because Joseph was the child of the woman he loved most.

Jacob showed more love towards Joseph than he did towards his other sons. He even made Joseph a special robe of many colors. His brothers thought this was totally unfair. They were jealous of their father's love for Joseph. Eventually, they did not like their brother very much.

Instead of talking to Joseph or their father about their feelings, the brothers kept it to themselves. This didn't solve things; it just made them more and more angry with Joseph. Soon their jealousy and insecurity began to poison their hearts. So they planned to get rid of Joseph, and lie to their father about what had happened.

God was not fooled, of course. He did not let the brothers get away with what they had done to Joseph. As the years went by, they fell into some really hard times. And, as far as we know, none of those brothers grew any closer to their father as a result of Joseph's disappearance.

After many years, Joseph and his brothers were reconciled. But just think of all the years they wasted — when they could have been bonding as brothers. Although

Jacob was glad that Joseph was still alive, it really must have hurt him to find out that his children had treated their brother so badly.

Don't make the same mistake. God loves His kids. He understands that no one likes to feel unimportant, and He wants to hear about what worries you. So please don't keep your fears to yourself. If you do, your *anxiety* will turn into *envy*. And envy is just heart pollution.

You should also talk to your parent about your fears. See if the two of you can come up with some ways to *stay connected*, just as you have always been. Do not put this off – things are calmer now than they will be when the baby arrives. Why not avoid the added stress and clear the air now?

If the new baby in your home has already arrived, don't worry; there is still time to have a heart-to-heart with your parent. Talk things out as soon as you can — you don't want that heart pollution to pile up inside you.

Give it time. God has created your family with every one of you in mind. Of course, not every day will feel like a blessing ... but trust God. He is in control, and His plans for you are good.

TALKING WITH GOD

Lord Jesus, I really want to feel excited about the new baby; but sometimes I feel jealous instead. My parent has been really distracted lately. I know I should try to understand, but I feel like I'm not as important anymore. Lord, help me to explain things to my parent so that my fear won't turn to envy. Please help me to feel love and joy for my new brother or sister. Amen.

MAKING CONNECTIONS

Your mother may not have been married at the time of your birth. You may have wondered how God feels about your birth, since your parents were never married. It could be that she was not yet a Christian at that time, and did not know or believe what the Bible says about saving sex for marriage. Or perhaps she went through a stage in life when she fell away from God's word. True, God did not want your mother to have a child outside of marriage, but God planned for you to be on this earth, and He loves you. If you are a believer, then it no longer matters how you arrived. It only matters that you are here and that you will live your life for God, believing in Jesus as your Savior.

DIGGING DEEPER

"But when his brothers saw that their father loved (Joseph) more than all his brothers, they hated him and could not speak peaceably to him," *Genesis 37:4.*

"They said to one another, 'We are truly guilty concerning our brother, for we saw the anguish of his soul when he pleaded with us, and we would not hear; therefore this distress has come upon us," *Genesis 42:21.*

"Let each of you look out not only for his own interests, but also for the interests of others," *Philippians 2:4.*

WEARING DIRTY LAUNDRY

Plunk. The note flew through the aisle like a tiny yellow airplane, then landed at Serena's feet. Serena carefully stretched her leg into the aisle, sliding the note under her desk. She let the note lay there a moment, making sure that her teacher had not seen the exchange. Then she pretended to drop her pencil so she could snatch the note into her hand.

The tiny yellow airplane was from Serena's friend, Alison. Alison always used her yellow notepaper when she had something shocking to report. It was her version of 'priority mail.' Sometimes the news was about Alison's own life; but usually it was a rumor she had heard about somebody else.

Once in awhile, Serena felt guilty when she read the latest from Alison. Her older sister, Samantha, had always taught her that gossiping was wrong. But then Serena smiled. Alison was really good at finding out the latest dirt. Most of it was true, too. Sometimes Alison's news was off a bit, but it was still fun to read. Anything was better to read than her calculus textbook.

Today's news flash was about Stephen Murphy. Stephen had serious dandruff issues, and his worn-out clothes usually had some bleach stains. He smelled like he was not a big fan of soap. He tried to be friendly to people; but he usually got shot down in flames:

Stephen, that is one nice shirt, bro! Where can I get one?

Hey, it's snowing! Oh, wait — Stephen was nodding his head.

Serena read the note. "Stephen Murphy Alert!!! Flake Boy is planning to go to Prom. He told Rob West that he would ask someone today before lunch! Rob thinks it will be Joanna Matthis. Stephen is such a tool!" To emphasize her insult, Alison drew a picture of a screwdriver, wearing a suit with bleach stains on it.

Serena covered her mouth to keep from laughing out loud. Her teacher raised an eyebrow. "Something to share, Serena?" she asked in an irritated tone. Serena sat up

WEARING DIRTY LAUNDRY

straight, covering the note with her arm. "No. I'm sorry. I just had to clear my throat," Serena lied. Out of the corner of her eye she could see Alison smirking.

Serena began to pay attention to the lesson. As she looked up at the board to take notes, she noticed the back of Stephen's flaky head. *He's a nice kid, I guess. Nasty appearance - but nice*, she thought. Serena figured he had a right to go to Prom just like anyone else did. Still, she couldn't wait to pass along the Stephen Murphy alert.

After class, Serena stopped two friends at their lockers. She gave them the news about Joanna Matthis. Then Serena hurried off to find another friend. She felt a strange sense of power when she passed a good secret around.

In the bathroom, Serena overheard Joanna Matthis talking to one of her friends. "It isn't even true!" Joanna said, sounding as if she was going to cry. "Stephen doesn't even talk to me. Why do people start such mean rumors?" she asked her friend.

"Don't worry," said the other girl. "Derek will ask you to Prom, then you'll forget all about it."

"No," Joanna insisted. "Derek heard the rumor and actually believed I was going with Stephen. So he asked Kim instead!"

Serena felt terrible. Joanna sounded so upset; and in a way, it was Serena's fault. If she hadn't spread the rumor, then maybe Derek wouldn't have heard it in the first place. Still, it's Derek's fault that he believed it, Serena reasoned. And besides, Alison is the one who started the whole thing — how was I supposed to know it wasn't true? Still, Serena didn't feel so great about herself at that moment. She decided to talk it over with Samantha once she got home from school.

Samantha was buried in textbooks when Serena walked in. Serena approached her slowly. "Sam, I need advice. Can you take a break?" she asked. Samantha let out a huge sigh. "Yeah, I'm having a mental block right now. I could use a break."

Serena told her about the note from Alison, and then the gossiping. Finally she told Samantha about Joanna's bathroom meltdown. Samantha frowned. "Serena, how would you feel if people were spreading stories about your life? I'm thinking you would hate it."

Serena nodded. "I would be angry. But I wasn't just making noise. I thought it was true."

This annoyed Samantha. "Weak defense, Serena. Even if it were a true story, you'd still be talking trash."

Serena knew that her sister was right. "But Sam, I just can't seem to help it. Gossiping is so much fun. When I get the inside scoop, I love being the one to spread it."

"Well, do you want complete strangers knowing all the

WEARING DIRTY LAUNDRY

dirt in your life — even if the dirt is true?" Samantha challenged.

Serena thought about all the things going on in her world that she'd never want to share. "Well ... no..."

"Then you shouldn't do it to other people," Samantha responded. "Now I have to get back to my paper."

The doorbell rang. Serena opened it. It was Stephen Murphy! "Hey, Serena," he said shyly. "Would you, ummm, wanna go to Prom with me?" he stuttered.

Oh, no! Serena thought. *The whole time, it was ME that he wanted to ask to Prom!* Even worse — right out on the sidewalk she saw Alison and two other girls walking home from school. They were watching the whole thing — and laughing. Alison mouthed, "Call me!" as she walked off with the girls. Soon the whole school would know. Alison would never keep a good story to herself — no matter who the story was about.

Serena turned back to Stephen. "I'm sorry, Stephen — but I'm not sure I even want to go to Prom. You should ask someone else." Stephen turned red. "OK, well, thanks," he mumbled. Then he shuffled away in his bleach-stained shirt.

Samantha opened her mouth to comment on the whole scene. Serena stopped her. "Please — I get it. What comes around goes around. I've just become 'priority mail'."

THINKING IT THROUGH

There is nothing worse than a painful or embarrassing moment – except maybe having that awful moment broadcast to the rest of the world. Everyone becomes the topic of gossip at one point or another. Sometimes it is true, and other times it's a complete exaggeration. Gossip brings fun and a feeling of power to the ones who spread it. But pain is no joke.

When people gossip about you, they rob you of your privacy. They also rob you of the chance to tell your own story. It is kind of like when someone stops by your house unexpectedly – but at that moment, everything is a mess. There are empty cans and wrappers everywhere, a pile of clothes on the sofa and papers scattered across the table. You are also wearing your oldest pajamas – the ones with a pizza stain and a big hole in the knee. In reality, you may have been studying hard for a huge test, and doing your laundry in between chapters. If you knew that they were coming, you definitely would have cleaned up first. But since they are looking in uninvited, they see the house at its worst, and they make their own assumptions. From the outside looking in, it appears that you are nothing but a slob.

This happened to Joanna when Serena spread the rumor about Stephen Murphy. When Derek heard the rumor that Joanna was going to Prom with Stephen, he chose to assume that the rumor was true. He never gave Joanna the chance to explain what really happened.

The same thing happened to Stephen. Rob assumed that Stephen would be asking Joanna to Prom. Rob didn't have all the facts. But he didn't ask Stephen for the rest of the story — and he did not keep Stephen's secret to himself. Instead, Rob chose to make up his own version of the story.

Before you share the details of another person's world, there are some things you should consider. First, are you sure that the information is true? The Bible warns us against spreading lies. If you were not there when it happened, or you have not spoken directly to the people involved, chances are that some of the details are wrong.

Next, are you being helpful to the person or people that the news is about? Thinking back on Serena's situation, no one was helped. When Serena first read Alison's note, she had a choice to make: she could keep the information to herself, or she could pass it on. Since Serena chose to pass it on, she was making a choice to be part of hurting other people.

Think about the fall-out from that rumor. Alison and Serena were distracted from schoolwork. Stephen was the subject of a joke, just because of his appearance. Derek was fooled. Joanna lost a date. All the people in the gossip chain had a part in causing the harm.

Finally, is it really necessary to spread the information along? Maybe you are positive that the story is true. It's possible that your reasons for spreading the story have nothing to do with power, or making fun of someone. Maybe you honestly believe that if other people knew, they could help.

Christians often make this mistake. They hear someone is having a problem then they ask others to pray for that person, telling them all the details involved. Meanwhile, the one who is hurting gets wounded all over again — this time from being forced into the spotlight.

If you really want to help someone by sharing a story with others, you must make sure that it is all right with that person. It is their experience. They own that life experience, and they have a right to privacy if they want it.

Sometimes the best thing you can do is spend time with that person, one-to-one. If they are up for it, pray with them or give them advice. What would you want if you were going through the same situation? Treat this person how you would like to be treated.

TALKING WITH GOD

Dear Lord, I have a problem with gossip. I know it is wrong, but sometimes it can be so much fun to talk about other people. As soon as I start to spread a rumor, I feel bad — but I don't always stop gossiping. I know you want me to stop, Lord. Please forgive me. Help me to think about how I would want to be treated if someone were talking about me instead. Amen.

MAKING CONNECTIONS

What about celebrity gossip? We sure don't want our own dirty laundry in the spotlight. Yet many people love to learn about the secrets and scandals in their favorite celebrities' lives.

Is it wrong to read magazines or watch television shows that 'tell all'? To figure this out, apply the same three words: truthful, helpful and necessary. For instance, a story about a star's messy break-up is not helpful to anyone — the star, her family, or the audience. In fact, it may be hurting a lot of the people involved to have their pain publicized.

It is not necessary for you to learn the details of the break-up in order to go about your day. And there is no way that you can know whether the details are true — it's not as if you can call her and ask.

On the other hand, if a celebrity is interviewed about her favorite workout routine, or her training for the Olympic medal, then it is more likely to be true, since the information is coming directly from her. It is helpful to her if you pass it along, because more people will know that she is a hard worker and cares about her health. Although it is not completely necessary to pass it on to others, maybe you have some friends who can benefit from her positive story and workout routine.

Begin to take notice of the things you listen to and read throughout your day. Then start to filter out the stuff that is not true, helpful or necessary.

DIGGING DEEPER

"A talebearer reveals secrets, but he who is of a faithful spirit conceals a matter," *Proverbs 11:13*.

"He who guards his mouth preserves his life, but he who opens wide his lips shall have destruction," *Proverbs 13:3*.

"Therefore, whatever you want men to do to you, do also to them," *Matthew 7:12*.

THE PARTY'S OVER

Mark helped his parents carry their luggage down the front steps. They were heading to Hawaii for their anniversary. Uncle Ray would be staying with Mark while his parents were away. Mom went through her list of emergency information as if Mark was an infant. She finally got into the cab. Mark waved, watching anxiously as they drove away.

As soon as the taillights were out of sight, Mark called his friend Duane. "They're gone!" Mark announced. "Start bringing over the stuff for the party right now!"

"Are you sure?" Duane asked. "Shouldn't we at least wait until the plane leaves?"

"No," Mark insisted. "We have to hide everything

before my uncle gets here. He's finished work in about an hour."

Mark hung up with Duane and looked around. He had to find a place to put all the stuff that Duane and the guys were bringing: a full sound system, including some wicked-loud speakers, a stellar music collection, and a video game system. He decided to make room in the basement.

Soon Duane was at the door, holding a bag that contained a few bottles of his father's whiskey stash. "Dude! This is gonna be so awesome!" Duane shouted. Mark agreed. He'd never had a party in his house before. He was planning to throw this one tomorrow night, while Uncle Ray worked graveyard shift. He wouldn't be home until 5:30 a.m., which would leave Mark plenty of time to get rid of the evidence. And Mark's parents would not be back for a full week.

Mark tried to ignore the guilt swimming around in his brain. Duane's bag of bottles made a loud clinking sound. Mark hurried him in to the house before the neighbors suspected anything. Then he motioned for the rest of the guys to bring the stuff from Duane's car. They followed him down the basement steps.

Mark moved some old boxes to the side. They put the speakers in the corner and then covered them with an old blanket. Then they hid some stuff in an empty carton. Just

THE PARTY'S OVER

as they were hiding the last of it, they heard a shout. "Mark?" Uncle Ray called. "Where are you, Bud?"

"I'll be right up," Mark yelled back. His heart was racing. "Let's go!" he whispered to the guys, pointing to the stairs.

When Mark got back upstairs, Uncle Ray looked surprised. "Hey! What are you guys doing in that old dirty basement?"

"Oh, we thought we'd surprise Mark's parents and clean it up while they were away," Duane volunteered. *Great*, thought Mark. *Not only will I have to clean the whole kitchen and living room after the party, but now I have to clean the basement, too!*

Uncle Ray looked pleased. "That's so cool, you guys! Need any help?"

"NO!" Mark answered, a little too quickly. "I mean ... it's really disgusting down there. And besides, we really want to do it ourselves. Like maybe tomorrow night," he lied.

After the guys left, Mark just wanted to go to his room. He had a lot of things to do – people to invite, plans to make. But more than that, he did not want to talk with Uncle Ray. He really liked his uncle – but it felt weird to spend time with him since he'd just told him a major lie. As Mark headed to his room, Uncle Ray stopped him. "Something wrong, Bud?" he asked.

"No," Mark lied again, "I've just been doing a lot of homework, and I'm tired."

"Oh, OK," Uncle Ray said. "Maybe you should get some rest, then."

This is bad, Mark thought. *This party thing requires a serious amount of lying.*

When Uncle Ray left for work the next afternoon, he questioned Mark again. "Mark, is something wrong? You've been really quiet all day."

"No, everything is great," Mark said. "Sorry I've been quiet. I've got a girl issue," he lied. He knew that would be a good excuse for being quiet.

Uncle Ray smiled. "Oh — I get it," he said. "Well, I'm here for you, Bud. You'll be sleeping long before I get home from work - but we can talk tomorrow."

Nice. Now I have to make up a girl problem tomorrow. More lying, thought Mark. *Please, just leave already!*

"That would be cool," said Mark. "I'll probably go to bed early. I have a headache," he said. At least the headache part was true. He was so stressed about the party that he felt like he had a brain tumor.

When Uncle Ray left, Duane and the guys brought over tons of junk food and a trillion cans of soda. They also had five huge bags of ice. "Where will we put all that ice?" Mark asked.

THE PARTY'S OVER

"Most of it can go in the bathtub," Duane answered.

"The bathtub?!" exclaimed Mark. "Great. Now I'm going to have people partying all over the house!"

"Don't worry!" Duane assured him. "We'll help you clean up afterwards."

Soon people started to arrive. Kids that Mark had never seen before were turning up loaded down with cans and bottles. A group of girls started searching the kitchen cupboards for bowls and cups. Two jocks started mixing drinks for the girls. One of them greeted Mark.

"Hey Dude — whose house is this? Does the kid go to our school or something?"

Mark was annoyed. "That would be me. Who are you?"

"No need to trip," said the other jock. "We were invited."

"Interesting," said Mark. "You were invited — yet it's my party, and I know I didn't invite you. So who did?"

One of the girls chimed in. "Sweetie, it's a party. Everyone invites everyone. It's not about you."

Mark was not happy. *This is way over the top*, he thought. The music was blasting. Food and drinks were spilled all over the rug. People were either laughing or arguing, and there was no room to move.

Suddenly, there was a pounding on the front door.

"POLICE!" a deep voice yelled.

Like a herd of wild animals, party guests shoved each other toward Mark's back yard so they could hop the fence. Others hid in rooms and closets. Some girls started crying. Two puked all over the furniture.

Mark walked quickly to the front door. When he opened it, a very large cop peered into the living room.

"Your neighbors are complaining of loud music. Are you having a party in here?" asked the cop.

"Well, we were ... but we're going to end it now," Mark answered.

The cop was not satisfied. "How old are you, son?" he demanded.

My life is over, Mark thought. "I'm eighteen," he lied, hoping that would keep the cop from calling his uncle.

"You're eighteen, huh?" said the cop. "Then you know that you can go to jail for giving alcohol to minors, correct?"

Mark hadn't thought of that. He had dug himself a hole with his own lie. "I meant, I'm sixteen," Mark said.

"Where are your parents?" the cop asked.

"Hawaii," answered Mark, wishing he were there right now too. "My uncle is staying with me, but he's at work."

The cop wrote something down on a pad of paper. Then he said, "I'm going to need his phone number, son.

We need to call him."

"Do you have to? I'll kick everyone out right now, and I'll never do it again," Mark pleaded.

"Sorry, son. Underage drinking is a serious matter. Your uncle needs to know."

There was nothing Mark could do. He was busted. Mark knew how much this whole thing would hurt his parents and his uncle. They would never trust him again.

THINKING IT THROUGH

Rules can be rough. How is it fair that someone else gets to make the decisions about your life? You may think that if you were in charge, there would be a lot more fun, and a lot less rules.

It can be hard to wait for the time in life when you will be the one in charge of your home or work situation. It can be tempting to ditch the rule book when no one is looking. In those moments, you might feel like you have some power over your choices.

Mark felt exactly like that. Instead of the typical quiet and order he lived in with his parents, he craved friends and loud music. When he found out that his parents were going away, he started planning his own vacation – a vacation from the rules. But in order to have his freedom, he needed to work out a ton of deceptive details: hiding stuff, lying to Uncle Ray, lying to Uncle Ray again, and – oh, yeah – lying to Uncle Ray.

It is amazing how many details are involved in breaking the rules. You have to work hard to pull off deception. One lie leads to another, which leads to another, and another. Pretty soon you are running a mental triathlon just to keep your stories straight.

Some of the lies may be things that you've said. But some lies involve the things that you haven't said. Many people try to excuse this second kind of lie. Maybe you've heard these people in action. For example:

"You never actually asked me if I talked to him."

"Well, technically, I never said that John's parents would be home, Dad."

"My mom doesn't even know I skipped church ... so why tell her?"

In all of these cases, the person speaking knows that they are holding back information. More than likely, the information is about things they should not have been doing. Holding back information is another form of lying.

This exact thing happened to Jacob in the Old Testament. Jacob had a twin brother, Esau. The tradition at that time was that only the first-born son got his father's blessing. Since Esau was born a few minutes before Jacob, Esau should have gotten the blessing ... except in this case,

THE PARTY'S OVER

things were different. Before the twins were even born, God had given clear instructions to their parents, Isaac and Rebekah, that their younger son would rule over their older son one day. God specifically wanted Jacob to be the head of the family after Isaac died.

However, neither Isaac or Rebekah were paying attention to God. Isaac's favorite son was Esau, and he wanted Esau to receive the special blessing. Rebekah loved Jacob more than Esau, but instead of trusting God to carry out his plans, she and Jacob formed a plan to get around the rule about the first-born. Since Jacob's father couldn't see well, they decided to trick him into thinking that Jacob was Esau. Instant blessing!

The plan took a lot of work. Jacob and Rebekah had to wait for Esau to leave the house. Sound familiar?

Deception Number 1. Jacob would need to find the two best goats he could. Once he did that, Rebekah would use the goats to make stew, just like Esau would have made it.

Deception Number 2. Jacob had to put on his brother's clothes to trick his father. But that wasn't enough, because Jacob wasn't a hairy guy. Apparently his brother's body hair was like an overgrown field.

Deception Number 3. Jacob put hairy goatskins on his hands and on the back of his neck (talk about going to extremes!) After all this, Jacob took the doctored-up stew to his father, ready for the ultimate scam.

Deception Number 4. Jacob let his father feel his hairy hands and neck, smell his clothing and taste the stew.

Deception Number 5. Jacob flat-out lied, saying he was Esau.

Pretty intense plan – all to get around the rules!

Notice that it wasn't just Jacob's words that were deceiving. His actions were also misleading; they lacked integrity. Integrity means to be honest, fair and trustworthy so that people can count on you. Integrity affects your life in all areas – family, friendships, school, work and church. In other words, the way you live out your life is just as important as the things that you say. Integrity is so important that God made it part of the Ten Commandments: "You shall not bear false witness against your neighbor." False witness is anything you say or do (or avoid saying or doing) to deceive someone else on purpose. For example, if you are deceiving anyone to get around the rules, then you are bearing false witness.

A lack of integrity is a serious faith issue. Do you really love God with all your heart? Then His rules should be the most important ones of all. Christians must have the integrity to keep this commandment.

MAKING CONNECTIONS

So you've never had a party while your parents were away. Smart move. But your integrity still may need a boost. Take a few minutes to consider these questions:

• Do you ever tell someone "I'll call you," knowing that you never will?

• Do you ever avoid people's phone calls, rather than telling them how you really feel?

• When a teacher leaves the room for a minute, do you stop working – just because you can?

• If you make a mistake at work and the boss blames someone else, do you let the other person take the fall?

If you've answered 'yes' to any of these questions, then there's room for improvement. But here's the good news: now you know what to work on. God loved Jacob, and He helped him to become a person of integrity. God can do the same for you.

DIGGING DEEPER

"Jacob said to his father, 'I am Esau your firstborn; I have done just as you told me; please arise, sit and eat of my game, that your soul may bless me,'" *Genesis 27:19.*

"You shall not bear false witness against your neighbor," *Exodus 20:16.*

"... In all things showing yourself to be a pattern of good works; in doctrine showing integrity, reverence, incorruptibility, sound speech that cannot be condemned, that one who is an opponent may be ashamed, having nothing evil to say of you," *Titus 2:7-8*.

AUTHOR PAGE:
LISA STADLER

Lisa Stadler has experience with young people, teens and stepkids. Merging her gifts of writing and counseling, Lisa has developed this book to reach out to teenagers struggling with the problems, issues and conflicts of modern life. With the background and wisdom that God has given her throughout her life and through His word, Lisa helps young people to discover God's answers. She has finished her Masters in Biblical Studies and is now pursuing her PhD in Psychology. Lisa is passionate about biblical truth. Lisa says, "Over the years, God has shown me the importance of delivering the truth with sensitivity and compassion."

ISSUES THAT YOU CARE ABOUT

Here are some books on the issues that affect you and your world.

Tlk 2 Me

Rachel Hall-Smith

RU there God? Listen to God's answer, 'I luv u'. Mobile phones are part of life today. But make God's text – the Bible – the centre of your life.
ISBN: 978-1-85792-822-8

Which Way You Gonna Jump?

Donna Vann

Star realizes that Ebony needs her friendship. But it's Ebony's mother's letters that bring both girls to realize that skin color doesn't matter to Jesus.
ISBN: 978-1-85792-368-1